LAFAYETTE

THE VIKINGS

With special thanks to Kevin Uhalde,
doctoral candidate in the
Department of History, Princeton University,
for his helpful reading of the manuscript.

Cultures
of the Past

THE VIKINGS

Kathryn Hinds

BENCHMARK BOOKS

MARSHALL CAVENDISH

NEW YORK

To Mom and Dad
AND, AS ALWAYS, HUGE LOVING THANKS TO ARTHUR AND OWEN

Benchmark Books
Marshall Cavendish Corporation
99 White Plains Road
Tarrytown, New York 10591-9001

© Marshall Cavendish Corporation 1998

Library of Congress Cataloging-in-Publication Data
Hinds, Kathryn, date.
    The Vikings / Kathryn Hinds.
        p.   cm.— (Cultures of the past)
    Includes bibliographical references and index.
    Summary: Describes the history, culture, and exploits of the Vikings and discusses their impact on the civilization of the British Isles and Europe in the eighth and ninth centuries.
    ISBN 0-7614-0271-3 (lib. bdg.)
    1. Vikings—Juvenile literature. 2. Northmen—Juvenile literature. [1. Vikings.]   I. Title.
II. Series.
DL65.H56   1998
948'.022—dc20   96-31067

Printed in Hong Kong
Photo research by Barbara Scott

Front cover: A Viking wood carving depicts weapon smiths making a sword for the legendary hero Sigurd. (Universitetes Oldsaksamling, Oslo/Werner Forman Archive/Art Resource, NY)
Back cover: Meeting of Althing at Thingvellir by W. G. Collingwood

POEM, page 48: translation by W. H. Auden and Paul B. Taylor, *Norse Poems,* p. 156

Photo Credits
Pages 6-7: Nasjonalgalleriet, Oslo/photo, J. Lathion/© Nasjonalgalleriet; back cover, page 52: The British Museum, Department of Prints and Drawings; page 8: Leo de Wys, Inc/V. Lefteroff; page 10: Royal Library, Sweden/*Codex Aureus;* page 12: The Pierpont Morgan Library, New York (M.736, f.9V); page 14: Berlin (West), Staatsbibliothek Preussischer, Kulturbesitz, Handschriftenabteilung/Ms. Hamilton 150, Bd 1, Bl, 177v; page 15: National and University Library of Iceland; pages 16, 37, 43, 57, 64: Statens Historiska Museum, Stockholm/Werner Forman Archive/Art Resource, NY; page 17: National Museum, Copenhagen/Werner Forman Archive/Art Resource, NY; pages 20-21: Art Resource, NY/Erich Lessing; pages 22, 23: Robert Harding Picture Library/David Lomax; page 23 *(inset):* Leo de Wys, Inc./J. Messerschmidt; page 25: University Museum of National Antiquities, Oslo, Norway (image of wooden wagon); pages 26-27: Robert Harding Picture Library/Martyn Chillmaid; page 28: Forhistorisk Museum, Moesgård, Norway; page 30: Universitetes Oldsaksamling, Oslo/Werner Forman Archive/Art Resource, NY; page 31: University Museum of National Antiquities, Oslo, Norway/Eirik Irgens Johnsen (image of academic head); page 32 *(top):* Knudsens-Giraudon/Art Resource, NY; page 32 *(bottom):* Ancient Art & Architecture Collection; page 34: Central Board of National Antiquities, Stockholm, Sweden/Bengt A. Lundberg; pages 36, 39: Werner Forman Archive/Art Resource, NY; pages 40, 42, 51, 55: Stofnun Árna Manússonar; page 45: Giraudon/Art Resource, NY; page 47: Manx Museum, Isle of Man/Werner Forman Archive/Art Resource, NY; page 48: Viesti Associates/Vladpans; pages 60-61: Robert Harding Picture Library/Jarlshof; page 63: The Slide File; page 65: The Restoration Workshop of Nidaros Cathedral, Trondheim, Norway; pages 66-67: Tom Till Photography/Tom Till; page 69 *(top and bottom):* Bob Krist.

CONTENTS

CHAPTER ONE

RAIDERS AND TRADERS

Almost everyone has heard of the Vikings: tall, blond, barbarian warriors from the far north of Europe, who wore horned helmets and sailed in dragon-headed ships. This popular image is

only part of the picture, however—and it's not entirely accurate. For one thing, the Vikings never wore horned helmets. More importantly, their culture was far richer than their reputation as primitive barbarians suggests. They were indeed warriors, but they were also merchants, explorers, settlers, farmers, craftspeople, storytellers, and poets. Daring and skillful sailors, the Vikings traveled the entire world known to medieval Europe. Everywhere they went they made a strong, and often lasting, impact.

A Viking fleet (shown here as a nineteenth-century artist imagined it) sets sail from Norway.

Masters of the Sea

In the year 793 Viking raiders attacked and plundered the monastery of Lindisfarne in the English kingdom of Northumbria. Without warning, the Viking Age in western Europe had begun. "Never before has such terror appeared in Britain as we have now suffered," wrote the Northumbrian scholar Alcuin, "nor was it thought that such an inroad from the sea could be made."

The Vikings, however, were masters of the sea. Their homeland was the northern European region known as Scandinavia, which occupies two peninsulas and hundreds of islands. In many areas of Scandinavia mountains, dense forests, and marshes made much land travel impossible. Waterways, on the other hand, were abundant and were taken advantage of from very early times.

Scandinavian raiders, merchants, and settlers had been voyaging from their home ports off and on for almost a thousand

In the year 834 a high-ranking woman was buried at Oseberg, Norway, in this superbly designed ship. Archaeologists think that it was probably a "royal yacht," used for ceremonial occasions and for traveling in sheltered waters.

In Viking Age Scandinavia, the word *viking* described an action, not a person: "To go a-viking" meant to sail away on a raiding expedition. The term may have come from the word *vik,* which meant "creek" or "bay," suggesting the sheltered waters from which Viking pirates set sail or in which they hid to prepare their lightning-swift attacks. Or it may have referred to the *wics,* the trading settlements that were often the targets of Viking raids. Another possibility is that the word *viking* came from *vikja,* meaning "going away" or "leaving home."

European and Arab writers, whose works have given us much of our information about the Vikings, called the Scandinavian raiders by many names: Northmen, Danes (even when they were from Sweden or Norway), Rus, Varangians, heathens, and barbarians. Only in the nineteenth century did historians begin to call them Vikings. Today we use the term Viking Age to describe the period of history from the eighth to the eleventh centuries, when Scandinavian raiders were most active. Sometimes, for convenience, all Scandinavians of that era are now referred to as Vikings, even though most of them never took part in a single raid.

years. They had already developed ships that were advanced far beyond those of any other European society. At the end of the eighth century the trickle of adventurers turned into a flood. There were many reasons for this. Conditions in Scandinavia were changing. The population had increased, and good farmland was becoming scarce. Only the oldest son could inherit a family's property, so younger sons had to go out to seek their fortunes. Political struggles were more and more common as the kingdoms of Denmark, Norway, and Sweden began to take form; defeated or out-of-favor leaders and their followers were often forced to leave their homelands. And loot and glory gained abroad gave men power when they returned home.

In western Europe, too, governments were often in turmoil, loosely organized and changing frequently. The political instability made many areas extremely vulnerable to attack. At the same time, a period of great economic growth had brought new prosperity to Europe. By the beginning of the ninth century there were many wealthy trading centers along coasts and rivers—tempting prey for sea-borne raiders.

The Fury of the Northmen

At first Viking raids were isolated incidents. The most frequent targets were monasteries on the coast of Ireland, which were not only places of worship and learning but also centers of art, crafts, and trade. In the 830s

Viking activity increased dramatically throughout Europe. Coastal and riverside towns and monasteries in England, Frankia (modern-day France and western Germany), and Frisia (today's Netherlands) became common prey. For example, beginning in 834 Vikings pillaged the great Frisian trading center of Dorestad four years in a row.

This ornate Bible manuscript was part of the loot that Viking raiders took from an English monastery in the ninth century. An English nobleman and his wife paid the Vikings a large sum of gold to have the book returned to Christian hands.

The Vikings, or Northmen as they were usually known, struck terror throughout the countries they attacked. They not only carried off valuables but also people, whom they held for ransom or sold into slavery. What they could not take away they often vandalized or destroyed. They did not hesitate to kill unarmed monks, women, children, and elderly people.

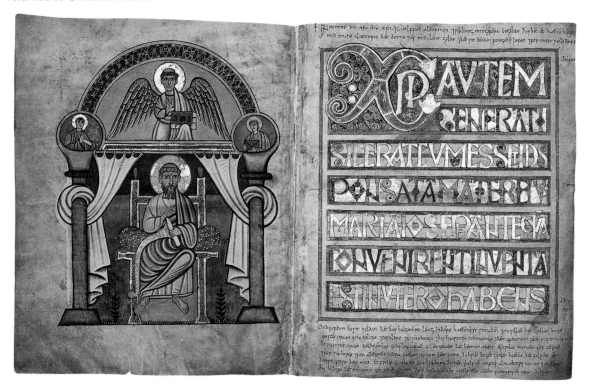

This kind of violence was not uncommon in Europe at that period but, to their victims, the Vikings seemed to carry it to a great extreme. The fact that the Northmen were not Christians and did not respect the holiness of churches and monasteries made the raids especially horrifying to the people of Christian

Europe. The attacks were all the more terrifying because of their unexpectedness and lightning swiftness.

Scandinavians had such superior skills in ship-building and sailing that other European communities were totally unprepared for what the Vikings could do. By the time a Viking ship or fleet was sighted, there was no chance to prepare a defense before the raiders landed. And by the time a counterattack could be launched, the Northmen were already back in their ships, sailing away.

By the middle of the ninth century hardly any place in Europe was safe from the Vikings. In 844 a fleet voyaged as far south as Muslim-ruled Spain, sacking Lisbon, Cadiz, and Seville. Elsewhere the Northmen were sailing ever farther inland. Great cities such as London, Paris, and Hamburg were ravaged. Vikings even raided in Scandinavia itself.

A helmet from seventh-century Sweden. Some Viking helmets were probably similar to this, while others were conical in shape.

The Vikings Settle In

In the early decades of the Viking Age the Northmen made raiding expeditions only in the summer months; when autumn came they sailed back to their homes. But in 839 Norwegian Vikings remained in Ireland for the winter, and in 841 they established a permanent settlement at Dublin. The next year Vikings wintered in Frankia for the first time, on an island near the mouth of the Loire River. From such bases the Northmen continued to head out on raids. More and more, however, they sought land to settle on, where they could farm and raise their families.

Vikings in the British Isles

By the middle of the ninth century, Norwegian Vikings were well established in northern Scotland, especially in the Shetland and Orkney Islands. Probably during the same period they were colonizing the Isle of Man in the Irish Sea. Some settlements were also made in southwest Wales.

In 866 a huge Viking force landed in England. This was known as the Great Army; it numbered as many as one thousand men, mostly Danes. The year after its arrival the army besieged

A twelfth-century English history shows Ivar the Boneless leading the Great Army's invasion of England in 866. Ivar became the first Viking ruler of York.

and captured York, the capital of Northumbria. The kingdoms of east Anglia and Mercia fell to the Great Army in the 870s. Only Wessex, England's southernmost kingdom, was able to resist the invasion, thanks to the strong leadership of Alfred the Great, king of Wessex.

During its first ten years in England the Great Army roamed the country during the summers, fighting and looting along the way, and spent the winters in various fortified camps. But in 876 one of the commanders, Halfdan, divided Northumbria among his men, who settled down to farm. In the next few years Mercia and East Anglia were shared out to other divisions of the Great Army. In a treaty of 886 Alfred the Great formally ceded most of these areas to the Northmen.

York and Dublin

The large portion of eastern and northern England that was under Viking control became known as the Danelaw. Its raiders-turned-farmers were soon joined by numbers of new Danish immigrants. The Danelaw's greatest center was York, which commanded England's major north-south land route. Crafts and trade flourished there, and merchants from all over the Viking world flocked to the town. It quickly became the heart of the Viking Kingdom of York.

In 902 Alfred the Great's son and successor, Edward, began to reconquer the Danelaw. Meanwhile the Norwegian Vikings of Dublin were driven out of Ireland, and many of them migrated to York. The Vikings returned to Dublin in 917, refounding the city on the site it still occupies today and building it into a prosperous trading center.

As Dublin rose, the Danelaw was falling. In 917 Edward and his sister Aethelflaed, queen of Mercia, decisively defeated the Northmen. By the next year only the Kingdom of York remained under Danish control—but not for long. Rognvald, the Norwegian ruler of Dublin, took over York in 919, and for several decades the kingdom repeatedly changed hands. The last Viking king of York was Erik Bloodax, killed in battle in 954.

Vikings in Frankia

Many members of the Great Army chose not to settle in England but went on to raid Frankia. In 911, tired of these attacks, the Frankish king Charles the Simple granted land near the mouth of the Seine River to a Viking leader known as Rollo (in Norwegian, Hrolf). In exchange, Rollo

The bishop of Rouen surrenders to Rollo. The fifteenth-century artist has depicted the Viking leader and his men in late-medieval armor, but in reality their only protection in combat would have been shields and helmets.

agreed to defend northern Frankia from other Vikings, and for several years he and his men did so. Then Rollo began leading raids on Frankish territory himself. He greatly extended the region under his control, and his son continued this process. The area settled by Rollo's Northmen was named Normandy after them. Rollo's descendants, who became Christians, ruled as the dukes of Normandy for generations and played important roles in European history.

Rollo also helped a large Norwegian army conquer Brittany (now part of France) in 914. But the Norwegians in Brittany never settled down to farm or trade. They simply continued to plunder the region until the Bretons at last drove them out in 939. That was the end of large-scale Viking activity in Frankia, although isolated raids occurred into the eleventh century.

To the Edge of the World

In the second half of the ninth century a large number of Norwegians, along with many Vikings who had first settled in Scotland and Ireland, sailed for new lands in the North Atlantic. Not only did they have to face the dangers of the rough sea, but they also had to brave the isolation and hardship of life on rugged islands with limited farmable land. But for a great many, the risks were well worthwhile.

Earliest to be colonized were the Faeroe Islands and Iceland. Iceland's first permanent settlement was founded around 870 by Ingolf Arnarson. By 930 some twenty thousand people had come to the island and were farming and raising livestock on the fertile lands of the coasts and river valleys. The settlements thrived, and Iceland became a proud, prosperous, self-governing nation.

In 982 a hot-tempered settler named Erik the Red was convicted of manslaughter and banished from Iceland for three years.

He had heard tales of some new land to the west and decided to find it and spend his exile there. So it was that Erik came to the huge island that he named Greenland. When he returned to Iceland he recruited twenty-five shiploads of settlers to join him in colonizing the new land; fourteen of them made it. Erik, the former outlaw, became Greenland's leading citizen.

To most Europeans, Greenland was at the end of the world. But in 986 an off-course Norwegian seafarer named Bjarni Herjolfsson (BYAR-nee HEHR-yolf-suhn) happened upon land even farther to the west. Intent on reaching Greenland, however, he never went ashore.

Around the year 1000 Erik the Red's son Leif (LAYF), who had inherited his father's spirit of adventure, set out to find the land sighted by Bjarni. He was successful and became the first known European to set foot in North America. Leif and his crew spent the

This fairly accurate sixteenth-century map of Iceland shows forty Viking settlements. It also shows the rugged terrain of mountains and glaciers (labeled Iokul) *that made the island's farmland so precious.*

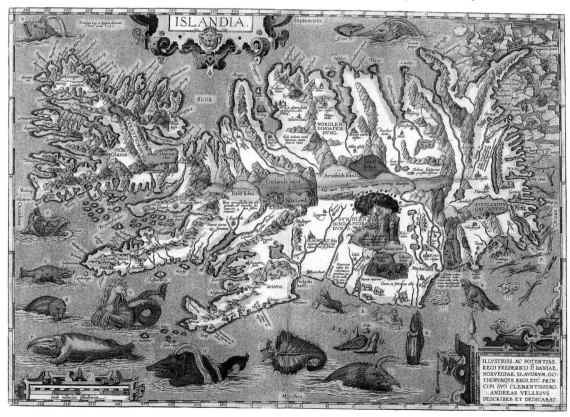

winter in a region he named Vinland, which scholars now believe was Newfoundland, Canada, and then returned home.

A few years later the Greenlander Thorfinn Karlsefni led three shiploads of colonists to Vinland and established a small settlement. At first relations between the Europeans and the area's Native Americans were friendly. But before long the settlers were fighting with the natives as well as quarreling among themselves. After three years they went back to Greenland. Although there were no more attempts at Viking settlement in North America, Greenlanders continued to travel there to obtain timber and furs well into the fourteenth century.

A VIKING SETTLEMENT IN NORTH AMERICA

Although several medieval Icelandic tales described Viking adventures in Vinland, for many centuries there was little evidence that the stories were true. Then in the early 1960s Norwegian explorer Helge Ingstad came to believe that the place the Vikings had called Vinland was Newfoundland, Canada. Ingstad and his wife, archaeologist Anne Stine, set out to prove his theory. Following local traditions that told of a group of buildings beside a brook at the northern tip of Newfoundland, they began to dig near the modern village of L'Anse-aux-Meadows. They discovered traces of several turf-and-stone houses with central hearths and side benches—very like the homes of many Viking settlers of Iceland and Greenland. There were also the remains of work sheds, cooking pits, and a forge, where iron rivets were made for use in boat repairs. Ingstad and Stine also found several Viking-style objects, including a bronze pin and part of a spindle (used by women to spin thread). These discoveries proved that the Vikings had indeed been the first Europeans to settle in the Americas.

The Profitable East

Most of the Vikings active in western Europe and the North Atlantic were Danes and Norwegians. The Vikings of Sweden directed their energies mainly eastward to the Baltic and Slavic lands that now make up eastern Germany, Poland, Lithuania, Latvia, Estonia, Finland, Russia, and Ukraine. In these areas they were usually known as the Rus (ROOS).

The Rus were warrior-merchants who traded furs, hides, down, walrus ivory, amber, nuts, honey, beeswax, falcons, and slaves for silk, wine, fruit, spices, jewelry, glassware, and, above all, silver coins from the

Arab empire based in Baghdad. From trade centers such as the Swedish town of Birka and the island of Gotland, the Rus crossed the Baltic Sea, then followed one of several river routes to the Black Sea. At some places they had to take their ships out of the water and move them on rollers from one river to another or past dangerous rapids. But at the end of the long journey they would reach the splendid city of Constantinople (now Istanbul, Turkey), capital of the Byzantine Empire.

Occasionally the Rus were not content with what they could trade for in Constantinople's markets. Around 860 a large fleet of Rus pillaged the city and surrounding areas for ten days. Raids occurred again in 907, 941, and 944. To buy peace with the Rus, the Byzantine emperor granted them special trading privileges and free food, lodgings, and baths when they were in Constantinople. He also recruited many Scandinavian warriors to fight in his armies.

Some Rus made their way even farther east. By sailing the Volga River they could reach the Caspian Sea, cross it, and take their goods to Baghdad by camel caravan. They might stop at the great trading center of Bulgar on the middle Volga, where they could get merchandise not only from the Arab world but from as far away as China.

Many Rus settled at trading centers along the river routes, eventually merging with the native Slavic population. Their impact was nevertheless significant. Around 862 a Scandinavian named Rurik became ruler of Novgorod, a gateway to the trade routes. Under Rurik's heir, Oleg, the Rus center of power moved to Kiev on the Dnieper River, commanding the passage to Constantinople. The Rus state steadily expanded and became known as Russia. It was ruled by Rurik's dynasty until the sixteenth century.

The Final Blaze of Glory

The late tenth and early eleventh centuries were periods of great transition in Scandinavia. Political and economic changes led Danes, Norwegians, and Swedes alike to seek instant wealth in

One of Viking Age Scandinavia's most beautiful and valuable exports was amber, which is fossilized tree sap. Amber could be used for jewelry and other objects; here it has been carved into a figurine of one of the Scandinavian gods. Rus merchants traded in amber at markets in eastern Europe, Constantinople, and even Baghdad.

unstable England. Viking raids resumed there in the 980s with fierce intensity. Scandinavian kings and would-be kings often headed these plunderous expeditions. In 991, for example, Olaf Tryggvason led ninety-three shiploads of Vikings in ravaging the southeast of England. The loot he carried off helped him win the crown of Norway four years later.

In 1013 the Danish king Svein (SVAYN) Forkbeard invaded England and became its ruler. He died the next year, but in 1016 his son Knut (or Canute) took the English throne. Three years later Knut became king of Denmark as well. In 1028 he gained a large amount of territory in Norway and soon after extended his influence into Sweden.

Knut's empire was the largest realm ever ruled by a Viking. It was also one of the best governed, at least in England, where Knut lived most of the rest of his life. His rule was firm but fair, and he strengthened laws that supported individual rights. He had become a Christian in 1013 and pleased the English people by making many donations to churches and monasteries. Most of all, England was at peace throughout Knut's reign.

"PEACE IN EXCHANGE FOR GOLD!"

"Peace in exchange for gold!"

This was the offer that a Danish army made to the defenders of the English town of Maldon in 991. It was an offer the Northmen had made or accepted many times before, beginning in 845. In that year Charles the Bald, king of the West Franks, had paid seven thousand pounds of silver to a force of Danes to get them to stop ravaging Paris. The Vikings were quick to realize that demanding money in exchange for leaving a town in peace was a much easier and safer way to turn a profit than looting the town and fighting its people. By the end of the ninth century the Franks had turned over more than forty-four thousand pounds of silver and gold to the Northmen.

The defenders of Maldon, however, refused to pay the Vikings and bravely stood their ground. They were crushingly defeated, but their heroism has lived on in a famous Old English poem, "The Battle of Maldon."

The English government turned out to be less courageous. After the battle, King Aethelred paid the Danes 10,000 pounds of silver—which temporarily got them to leave but ultimately encouraged more and more Vikings to seek their fortunes in England. By 1014 the English had paid the Northmen more than 150,000 pounds of silver. These payments, which became known as Danegelds, were shared out among all the Viking warriors. Although the Danegelds drained England, they so enriched some Viking leaders that they were able to become kings when they returned home to Scandinavia.

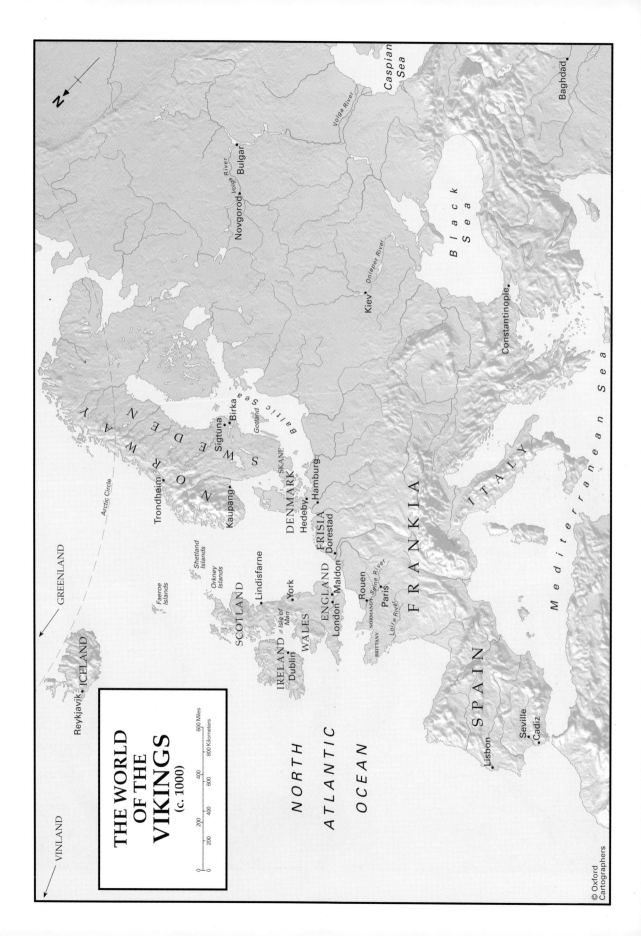

THE WORLD OF THE VIKINGS (c. 1000)

600 Miles
800 Kilometers
400
600
400
200
200
0
0

VINLAND

GREENLAND

Reykjavik ICELAND

Arctic Circle

NORWAY

SWEDEN

Trondheim

Kaupang

Sigtuna
Birka

Gotland

Baltic Sea

DENMARK
SKANE
Hamburg
Hedeby
FRISIA
Dorestad

Shetland Islands

Orkney Islands

Faeroe Islands

SCOTLAND

Lindisfarne

York

Isle of Man

IRELAND
Dublin
WALES

ENGLAND
London Maldon

Rouen
NORMANDY Seine River
Paris
BRITTANY
Loire River

FRANKIA

ITALY

SPAIN

Lisbon

Seville
Cadiz

Mediterranean Sea

NORTH

ATLANTIC

OCEAN

Novgorod
Volga River
Bulgar

Volga River

Dnieper River

Kiev

Black Sea

Constantinople

Caspian Sea

Baghdad

N

© Oxford
Cartographers

But after his death in 1035 his empire collapsed, and England's brief stability came to an end.

In 1066 the Viking Age reached its ultimate climax. In this year the king of Norway, Harald Hardradi (HARTH-rah-thee; "Hard Ruler"), invaded England. He was defeated by the English king Harold Godwinsson, the grandson of a Danish Viking, on September 25. Less than a month later Harold was defeated by William, Duke of Normandy (William the Conqueror). On Christmas Day William, a direct descendant of the Viking leader Rollo, was crowned king of England.

The events of 1066 mark the end of the Viking Age. Although there were occasional Norwegian raids on the British Isles into the thirteenth century, the great outpouring of Scandinavian raiders and traders was over. But the Vikings had made their mark, and in many places Scandinavian influence would remain strong for centuries to come.

Norman horsemen ride into battle in this scene from the Bayeux Tapestry. The tapestry, a 230-foot-long strip of linen, is embroidered with images of William of Normandy's conquest of England. It may have been made by William's wife, Matilda.

CHAPTER TWO

SHIPBUILDERS, ARTISTS, AND POETS

A replica of the "royal yacht" discovered at Oseberg demonstrates the seaworthiness—and beauty—of Viking ships.

Although the Viking Age is named for the adventurers who sailed out in search of trade, plunder, and new lands abroad, the majority of Viking Age Scandinavians remained at home. They lived more or less peaceful lives, supporting themselves primarily by farming and fishing. But all were affected by the Viking expeditions. Many people owned at least a few imported items, brought to Scandinavia either as trade goods or loot. Many had friends or relatives who had voyaged away, sometimes never to return. Scandinavia's increased contact with the rest of Europe brought about changes in everything from fashion to art to government and religion. All in all, the Viking Age was a time of great wealth, energy, and creativity for the Scandinavian people.

The Vikings on the Move

The intense level of Scandinavian activity abroad during the eighth to eleventh centuries was made possible by the masterfully crafted Viking ship. By the beginning of the Viking Age Scandinavian shipbuilders had invented and perfected the keel, which projected from the ship's bottom, down the length of its center, and formed its backbone. The hull, or ship's body, was built of overlapping planks of oak or pine, held together with iron rivets and caulked with tarred animal hair. This construction made the vessel incredibly flexible and at the same time very stable and watertight.

The Viking ship used a square or rectangular sail. It was steered by a large oar fixed to the right side of the stern. The right-hand side of a ship is still called starboard, from the Vikings' words for "steering board." A high, tapering prow and stern gave the Viking ship its distinctive look.

Modern reproductions of the two best-preserved Viking ships lie moored side by side in a Norwegian harbor.

Ships for Warriors and Merchants

The Vikings used two main types of ships. The first was built for war and travel, the second for transporting cargo. The warships were as long as one hundred feet and relatively narrow. Equipped with both sails and oars, they could be rowed when there was no wind or when greater maneuverability was needed. The mast could be lowered quickly and easily, which was useful for surprise attacks and for passing under bridges. Viking warships rode high in the water, so they could easily navigate rivers and could be pulled right up onto shore. Many of these vessels were magnificently decorated, with carved dragon heads or gilded bronze weather vanes on the prows and rows of painted shields hanging along the sides.

The Viking Ship Museum in Roskilde, Denmark, houses the remains of five ships that were found wrecked in a nearby inlet. Two were warships, two were cargo ships, and one was a fishing boat or ferry. The wrecks have helped archaeologists understand a great deal about Viking shipbuilding.

Seagoing cargo ships could carry huge loads of merchandise and were also used to transport settlers and their livestock. They were quite a bit wider than the warships and had higher sides. They had fixed masts and used oars only to maneuver in and out of port. Cargo ships could not draw up onto shore, so if a harbor had no docks or jetties, the ships had to be unloaded by small boats.

Trade on the river routes of eastern Europe required a somewhat different type of cargo ship, small and light enough to be drawn overland when necessary, and equipped with oars for negotiating the rivers. The remains of such a ship were discovered on the Baltic island of Gotland,

LIFE ABOARD A VIKING SHIP

Viking ships were beautiful and wonderfully seaworthy. But if you had sailed on board one, you probably would not have found it very comfortable.

Imagine that you are one of a shipload of settlers beginning the voyage from Norway to Iceland, eight hundred miles away. Manning the cargo ship's single pair of oars, sailors maneuver the vessel out of the harbor. Then the sail is raised, and you pray that a fair, steady wind will carry the ship quickly and safely across the North Atlantic. Depending on the winds and the sea, your journey will take anywhere from a week to a month.

At first the ship sails close to the Norwegian coastline. In the evening it puts in to land. Campfires are lit, cauldrons are hung over them, and everyone enjoys a hot meal. Then it's time to set up wood-framed tents to camp for the night. The leaders of your expedition may have finely carved travel beds, but you sleep in a two-person skin bag that was filled with gear during the daytime.

When the ship heads west into the open ocean, the hardships of the voyage begin. The sea may be dotted with icebergs, and the waves can be fierce. The ship has no cabins of any kind, so there is no protection from the elements, except perhaps for some skins or tent canvas stretched over a part of the ship. Sometimes you can't help worrying that the ship will sink or be wrecked.

Even if there are no storms and the sea is calm, you may start wishing for this voyage to end soon. You are cold and wet most of the time, and you have to eat cold food; no cooking can be done on board because of the risk of fire. The ship is extremely crowded, not only with sailors and settlers and all their supplies and belongings, but also with livestock, which the settlers will need on their new farms. There is no privacy, and no place to go to the bathroom except over the sides of the ship.

It is a relief to make a brief stop in the Shetland Islands, and then in the Faeroe Islands. Now you are more than halfway to your journey's end. The last stretch of open sea is the longest, but with good luck on your side, you will soon be starting life in your new home on Iceland.

and in the late 1980s a replica of it was built. Then, with a cargo of iron, a ten-man crew re-created a Rus trading expedition along the eastern European river route, sailing, rowing, and dragging the ship all the way from the Baltic Sea to Istanbul. The journey took three months.

Travel Inland and Overland

Travel in the Viking Age was naturally not limited to the great ships. In fact, most Scandinavian vessels of the time were small boats of various types, including fishing boats, ferries, and boats for traveling on inland lakes and rivers. Such boats made it easy for ordinary people to travel between settlements, visiting and exchanging news and local goods.

Land travel in Scandinavia was far more difficult than water travel. For example, traveling overland from Skane in southern Sweden to Sigtuna in central Sweden took a month, while the journey by boat took only five days. Nevertheless, land travel was often necessary. Most people simply walked. Only the wealthy rode horses. High-ranking women might drive horse-drawn wagons, which could be ornamented with elaborate carvings.

In many areas land travel was easiest in the winter, when bogs were frozen over and thick snow leveled rough terrain. On foot people used skis, snowshoes, and ice skates. The skates, which were more like very short skis than like the skates we know today, were made of bone and strapped onto the feet. Skaters used iron-tipped sticks, rather like ski poles, to propel themselves over the ice. Winter travelers with goods to transport might pull a small sled. Wealthy people could ride in horse-drawn sleighs.

This richly decorated wagon, carved with scenes from heroic legends, was one of the objects buried with a noblewoman in Oseberg, Norway.

The Vikings at Home

Most Viking Age Scandinavians lived on farms. In very fertile areas, including Denmark and southern and central Sweden, half a dozen or so farmsteads would cluster together in a village. In places with less fertile land, such as Iceland and western Norway, farms would be far apart from one another.

An average farmstead consisted of the house where the family lived and several smaller outbuildings. These could include workshops, storerooms, dwellings for servants and slaves, a cookhouse, and even a sauna. There might also be barns, but it was very common for cattle to have their stalls in one end of the main house. This arrangement protected the animals both from rustlers and from the extreme winter cold. The presence of the cattle inside the house also gave the farm family an extra source of heat.

The Scandinavian Longhouse

Viking Age houses were rectangular and could be as long as 150 feet. Depending on local conditions, they were built of wood, sod, or wattle-and-daub, roofed with thatch, turf, or wooden shingles. The roof was usually supported by two rows of posts inside the house. The floor was sometimes made of timber but more often of hard-packed earth, which might be spread with straw. The walls, which could be paneled on the inside with wood, had only a few tiny windows.

A typical Viking house was divided into three or more rooms, the smaller ones being used to store provisions. The largest room, in the middle section of the house, was the main living area. In the center of it was a raised hearth for heat, light, and cooking. Since there was no chimney (smoke filtered out through small gaps in the roofing), the house was always smoky. It was also fairly dark, for the only sources of light besides the hearthfire were oil lamps and perhaps candles.

Along each side of the living area were raised earthen benches faced with wood.

These might be covered with skins, furs, or rugs and cushions. It was on these benches that the members of the family slept at night and ate, worked, and socialized during the day. Generally a few low stools were the only other furniture. Shelves and lockable chests were used for storing utensils and personal items. Leaning against one wall was the loom where the women of the family wove cloth for clothing and sails.

A reconstruction of a farmhouse in Iceland. It is built entirely of turf, on stone foundations. The long hall, or living space, has two sections, each with a central hearth. The two rooms projecting out from the hall were probably used for processing milk products and wool.

The inside of a typical Viking Age house would have looked like this. In the center is the rectangular hearth. Next to the door is the house-wife's loom; the stone weights at the bottom keep the long threads taut.

The halls of nobles and kings would have been much like the houses of farmers. The aristocratic dwellings, however, were larger and probably were decorated inside and out with elaborately carved woodwork. Colorful tapestries hung on the interior walls, and the finely crafted furnishing included tables, chairs, and beds.

In the Towns

One of the most significant developments of Viking Age Scandinavia was the growth of towns. Before this era there had been seasonal market centers where people gathered now and then to carry on crafts and trade, perhaps for several weeks each summer. These markets, such as the one at Kaupang in Norway, continued to exist in Viking times. But increasing foreign trade required more permanent centers.

VIKING FASHIONS

In Viking Age Scandinavia most people's clothes were woven and sewn at home by the women of the family. Rich and poor wore similar styles of clothing, but the materials could be very different. The clothes of slaves and servants were made of coarse, undyed wool, while the well-to-do wore fine linen and colorfully dyed wool. Very wealthy people might even have garments of imported silk.

Viking women typically wore an ankle-length underdress of pleated linen, closed at the neck with a drawstring, a ribbon, or a small metal brooch. Their upper garment was a kind of apron or jumper that reached from the chest to midcalf. It was held in place by shoulder straps, which were fastened by a pair of large oval brooches. A string of beads might be hung between these brooches, and often sewing tools were fastened to chains suspended from them. Later in the Viking Age, influenced by fashions from Frisia and the Byzantine Empire, women added shawls to their costumes. The shawl was fastened with a brooch, too.

Men wore trousers and a belted tunic that reached to just below the hips. The trousers could be loose or tight and might be bound from knee to ankle with strips of cloth. Some men copied Eastern fashions and wore very baggy knee-length trousers. For an outer garment a man might wear a fur-trimmed jacket or, more commonly, a cloak that was fastened with a brooch on the right shoulder, leaving the sword arm free. Both men and women wore lowcut leather shoes. Men might also have ankle-high or calf-high boots; the finest were made of goatskin.

Perhaps the most distinctive thing about the Vikings' clothes was that they were relatively clean. Most Europeans of the time rarely bathed or changed their clothes. Scandinavians, however, were in the habit of taking a bath (sometimes a sweat bath or sauna) and changing their clothes once a week. They also took great care with their hair; combs were common and essential possessions. Far from being uncouth barbarians, Viking Age Scandinavians were actually the most well-groomed people of medieval Europe!

Most Viking Age towns were founded by kings or powerful landowners, who profited from taxes on the towns' imports and exports. Houses and streets, which might be paved with wood, were laid out according to plan. Towns had good, sheltered harbors and were often located where trade routes joined or crossed. In the tenth century, when their great wealth made them targets of both Scandinavian and Slavic raiders, these towns were fortified with high earth ramparts, often topped by wooden palisades.

Viking towns bustled with activity. Merchants came to them from all over Scandinavia and the rest of Europe, and even from the Arab world, to trade in raw materials and luxury items. Farmers from the surrounding countryside brought their surplus produce and bartered it for manufactured items such as soapstone cooking pots and combs made of antler. From town harbors, ships loaded with Scandinavian goods sailed for the trade centers of the British Isles, western Europe, and the East.

Still, these early towns were more like rural villages than like towns as we think of them today. The largest Viking town, Hedeby in Denmark, had only fifteen hundred residents at its height. Each family had a fenced-in plot with a main house and several outbuildings, one of which might be a store. Houses were not as long as those in the countryside, both because the towns were more crowded and because town dwellers did not need to keep livestock in their homes. The main difference between towns and villages was that town dwellers earned their living from crafts and trade instead of from farming.

One of the most respected craftspeople in the Viking world was the weapon smith. In this wood carving, which shows a scene from a popular Viking legend, weapon smiths work on a sword for the hero Sigurd.

A Vigorous Style

In the Viking world all artists and craftspeople were known as smiths. They made and sold their products in towns, were employed in the households of kings and nobles, or traveled from village to village to make or mend whatever was needed. One traveling smith was so unfortunate as to lose his toolbox in a bog on the island of Gotland. When archaeologists found it, it contained more than two hundred objects, including incomplete and finished products as well as tools for working wood, iron, and bronze.

The Vikings used art mainly for decoration, and even very functional objects might be highly ornamented. The art style was vigorous and unique, although the smiths did absorb influences from the British Isles, Frankia, and eastern Europe. Art in these areas, especially England, was in turn influenced by Scandinavian styles.

Fantastic Beasts

Viking designs could be complex and extremely detailed. They usually featured highly stylized animals. Ninth-century smiths favored "gripping beasts," animals that might look something like dogs, cats, lions, and/or bears, whose paws gripped themselves, neighboring animals, or other parts of the design. Some gripping beasts look almost like cartoon characters, while others are grotesque or even fearsome. A later stylized animal figure seems to be a cross between a lion, a deer, and a horse, with graceful tendrils for ears, mane, and tail. At the end of the Viking Age the animals tended to be thin and snakelike, intertwining with one another in complicated curves and loops.

Viking artists rarely portrayed human beings, but when they did it was in a fairly realistic fashion. This made a great contrast with the fanciful animal designs. Indeed, the Vikings loved contrast—in color, texture, and material, for instance in intricate silver designs on the black iron of a battle ax. Many objects of stone and wood were painted in strong colors, especially black, red, and white, but also blue, green, brown, and yellow.

This wonderfully carved wooden dragon probably snarled from the prow of a Viking warship, frightening enemies and protecting the ship and its crew from evil spirits.

Masterworks in Wood and Stone

Viking smiths worked in a wide variety of materials, including wood, stone, iron, gold, silver, bronze, ivory, whalebone, elk and reindeer horn, glass, and amber. Weapon smiths and ship smiths were the most highly respected craftspeople. Other smiths made everything from jewelry to harness fittings to tent poles to carved wall panels.

The Vikings' most distinctive artistic achievements were in wood and stone. Unfortunately, few wooden objects have survived the centuries. Some of the finest were discovered at Oseberg, Norway, where they had been buried with a high-ranking woman, possibly a queen named Asa. The woman was laid to rest in an elegant ship (see page 8), its prow and stern decorated with fine

31

carving. With her were many of the objects she had used during life, including a wagon (see page 25) and three sleds, all of them covered with elaborately carved scenes and designs. These findings give us a small taste of the great skill and creativity of Viking wood smiths.

On the island of Gotland smiths had been chiseling pictures onto large slabs of stone since the fifth century. The vivid scenes carved during the Viking Age are not only fascinating works of art but also tell us many things about life at that time. They portray ships in full sail, warriors in battle, episodes from mythology and

One of four carved male heads that were part of the supports for the bed of the Oseberg wagon. The neatly combed mustache and beard were typical of Viking men.

A tenth-century picture stone from Gotland. In the top panel two warriors wearing baggy eastern-style trousers engage in single combat. Below, a shipload of warriors in conical helmets hold their round shields at the ready.

heroic legends, and other subjects. Arranged in rows, the pictures often seem to be telling a story. The stones stood up to twelve feet high and were probably erected as memorials to the dead.

Around the middle of the tenth century artists in other parts of Scandinavia also began to carve pictures into stone. These were very different from the Gotland stones. They were much simpler, usually showing only one scene, of a person or stylized animals. Only rarely did the pictures tell a story. They were almost always accompanied by writing, which recorded notable deeds of people both living and dead.

Words to Remember

The Vikings wrote their language, Old Norse, with a unique alphabet called the futhark. Its letters were known as runes. Originally there were twenty-four runes, used by many of the Germanic peoples of Europe. By the Viking Age only Scandinavians were still using the futhark, and they had pared it down to sixteen runes. There is evidence that the runes were sometimes employed as magical symbols, but generally they were used for more ordinary communication.

The runes were composed mainly of vertical and diagonal lines because they were developed for easy carving on wood. They were also carved into bone, antler, metal, and, most notably, stone. All over Scandinavia, especially Sweden, and in some of the Viking colonies, large stones engraved with runic messages were set up where they would be seen by passers-by. In the early Viking Age the runes were usually carved on the stone in simple vertical bands. Later the runic inscription might frame a picture or be enclosed in the curves of a snakelike animal's body.

Rune stones were usually set up in memory of a dead friend or relative. An example of a typical inscription is: "Toki and his brothers raised this stone in memory of their brothers. One of them met his death in the west, and the other in the east." A rune stone could also commemorate an achievement or good deed of the person who had the stone raised. A magnificent Norwegian rune stone records, "Gunnvor, Thryrik's daughter, built a bridge in memory of her daughter Astrid. She was the most skillful girl in Hadeland."

Runes were used for many other purposes, especially for carving messages on sticks of wood. Smiths sometimes signed their works with

The carver of this Swedish rune stone followed the common practice of enclosing the runes in the curves of a snake's or dragon's body, but also took the opportunity to illustrate a famous legendary event: The great Scandinavian hero Sigurd appears at the top of the stone, plunging his sword into the belly of the dragon.

runic inscriptions, such as "Thorfastr made a good comb." People might engrave their belongings with runes: "Rannveig owns this casket." And in the far-flung places the Vikings traveled to, many left their mark in the form of graffiti, such as this inscription from a prehistoric burial mound in the Orkneys: "Ingigerd is the sweetest woman there is."

Poetic Traditions

The futhark was very practical in many ways—a Viking always carried a knife and could easily get a piece of wood or bone to carve a message on—but it was not very suitable for writing books. Instead, Viking Age Scandinavians memorized their poems, stories, histories, and laws and passed them on orally from generation to generation.

Poetry played an important role in Viking culture. It flourished especially in the royal and noble courts, where poets called skalds were richly rewarded. Skalds might live at one court or travel around to various courts. In honor of their aristocratic hosts they composed elaborate poems, which they recited at feasts and other gatherings. Skaldic poems, full of praise for great deeds and generosity, boosted a king's or noble's reputation and assured him of lasting fame.

The Vikings respected skaldic poetry as the highest of arts. The poems' style was extremely complex, using many unusual words, arranged in an order far different from that of ordinary speech. Because the poems were meant to be recited—they may even have been chanted or sung—the element of sound was very important. The poems were highly rhythmic and full of alliteration, a literary device that uses two or more words in a line beginning with the same consonant or vowel sound.

Skaldic poetry referred to all sorts of mythological and legendary people and events, often through expressions called kennings. In a kenning two nouns were combined to form a particular image of the thing being described. For instance, "burden of dwarfs" was a kenning for *the sky*—but listeners to the poem would understand it only if they knew the Scandinavian myth in which four dwarfs were said to hold up the sky. Many kennings did not require mythological knowledge but were more riddle-like than those that did. Among these were such expressions as "steed of the waves" for *ship*, "hail of weapons" for *battle*, and "sweat of the sword" for *blood*.

Such complexities were greatly appreciated by the skalds' aristocratic audiences. There were also simpler types of poems, which all levels of society probably enjoyed. These poems, too, were rhythmic and used alliteration, but they were fairly straightforward. They told stories of gods, goddesses, and heroes, and must have provided entertainment around many hearths during the long Scandinavian winters.

CHAPTER THREE

FROM CREATION TO DOOM

The Vikings held to an ancient belief system that had developed in tune with their environment and way of life. They honored many goddesses and gods, each having her or his own particular area of concern. This allowed worshipers to focus their prayers: Whether they sought victory in war, a successful voyage, the birth of a child, or a bountiful harvest, there was a deity to turn to in any situation.

Viking Age Scandinavians also acknowledged various kinds of nature spirits, both helpful and harmful. Dwarfs, who lived in the earth, were involved with the use of metals, especially iron and gold. Giants personified the raw forces of nature, such as cold, ice, and mountains. The light elves, on the other hand, were associated with sunlight and growth.

At one time many of these beliefs had been common to most of the Germanic peoples of Scandinavia and what are now England, Germany, and the Netherlands. But by the Viking Age only Scandinavia continued to follow the old religion; the rest of northern Europe had turned to Christianity. The new beliefs soon gained footholds in Scandinavia, too. By the time the Viking Age ended in the eleventh century, Christianity was the official religion of Denmark, Norway, Sweden, and the North Atlantic islands.

During the Viking Age Christianity came to Scandinavia and existed side by side with the native beliefs. Early Scandinavian churches, like this twelfth-century Norwegian church, were often decorated with carvings of scenes from Scandinavian myths. The buildings themselves may have been modeled on temples of the native deities.

In the thirteenth century a number of the old poems and stories about the gods and goddesses were written down. The poems were collected in a book known as the *Poetic Edda* or *Elder Edda*. In the *Prose Edda* or *Younger Edda* the great Icelandic writer Snorri Sturluson retold many Scandinavian legends in his own words. He was trying to help young poets understand the mythological roots of traditional poetry, for by this time people were forgetting much of the ancient lore. Snorri himself, along

The Vikings' most important gods were Odin, Thor, and Frey. In this twelfth-century Swedish tapestry, Odin carries an ax, Thor raises his hammer, and Thor and Frey together hold up an ear of grain. These three things symbolized war, protection, and plenty.

with the writers of the *Poetic Edda*, may not always have properly remembered or completely understood the old myths. Nevertheless, it is thanks to the *Edda*s that we are able to form such a full picture of the Vikings' ancient beliefs.

The Creation

In the beginning there was no heaven, earth, or sea, but only a great void. To the north of the void was a foggy world called Niflheim (NIH-fuhl-haym), to the south of it a fiery world called Muspell. Eleven rivers flowed out of Niflheim; when their waters reached the void, they froze. The ice that was nearest the sparks and flames of Muspell began to melt, and the thaw formed a giant named Ymir (IH-mir). In the heat from the fiery world, his sweat became a man and a woman, the first frost giants.

More ice thawed, becoming the cow Audhumla (OWTH-hum-luh), who began to lick the ice blocks surrounding her. After three days her licking uncovered a man, Buri. His son Bor married the giant Bestla, and their three sons were Odin (OH-thin), Vili, and Ve (VAY), the first gods. These three killed Ymir. They made the ocean out of his blood, the sky out of his skull, the earth out of his flesh, the mountains out of his bones, and the trees out of his hair. They threw sparks from Muspell into the sky to give light to their creation.

Odin, Vili, and Ve traveled over the new world. They came upon two trees, an ash and an elm. From these they created Ask and Embla, the first human man and woman. Odin gifted Ask and Embla with spirit and life, Vili gave them movement and understanding, and Ve contributed the powers of sight, hearing, and speech. Then the gods took the giant Ymir's eyebrows to enclose Midgard (MITH-garth), "Middle Earth," and gave this world to the man and woman and all their descendants.

The World Tree

The universe was supported by a great ash tree, Yggdrasil (IG-druh-sil). In its roots and branches were the nine worlds of fire, humans, dwarfs, light elves, dark elves, giants, the dead, the deities called the Aesir (EYE-sir), and the deities called the Vanir (VAH-nir). The tree had three roots, and under each was a spring, or well. One of these was the well of wisdom and another the well of fate. From the third spring came a serpent who gnawed constantly at the tree's nearest root.

A learned eagle perched in Yggdrasil's branches, and a squirrel ran up and down the trunk carrying messages between it and the serpent. Goats and deer nibbled on the leaves and new growth. Bees fed on dew that dripped from the tree, and swans drank from the well of fate. Beside that well lived the three Norns, immortal maidens who ruled over past, present, and future. The Norns drew water from their magical well every day and sprinkled it on Yggdrasil to keep it green and thriving, for all life depended on the World Tree.

This wall panel, carved late in the Viking Age, is thought to show Yggdrasil, the World Tree, with a deer feeding on its twigs and leaves.

The All-father and His Family

The highest of the gods was Odin. He fathered many children, all of whom were deities, and for this reason he was known as All-father. He and his family were the Aesir, and their realm was called Asgard (AHS-garth). There Odin had his high seat, from which he could see over all the worlds. There too was his great hall Valhalla, roofed with shields, where dead warriors came to feast with him. They were brought from earth's battlefields by the Valkyries (VAL-kih-rees), thirteen maidens who served the All-father.

Odin thirsted for knowledge. Every morning he sent out two ravens, named Thought and Memory, to fly through the world and gather news. When they returned they sat on his shoulders and told him all that they had seen and heard. But Odin desired deeper knowledge, so he gave up one of his eyes in exchange for a drink from the well of wisdom. Still he remained unsatisfied. He hung himself on Yggdrasil, wounding himself with his spear, and remained there for nine nights until at last the magical powers of the runes were revealed to him. That is how Odin became the Full-wise, master of every kind of knowledge.

Odin was a fierce, cunning, and mysterious god, worshiped by kings, warriors, and poets. He could grant victory and inspiration, but he was unpredictable. He often journeyed among humankind, disguising himself and taking on different names. In his travels he had relationships with a number of goddesses and female giants, but these never lessened his love for his wife, Frigg.

Frigg was the goddess of marriage, motherhood,

Odin's great hall Valhalla, as a medieval Icelandic artist imagined it. In the largest doorway Odin himself waits to greet the warriors slain in Midgard's battles. It was said that Valhalla had 540 doorways so that 800 warriors, side by side, could enter at once. Above the towers a stag and a goat browse on the leaves of the World Tree.

THE MEAD OF POETRY

There was a man named Kvasir (KVAH-sir), made from the mixed spit of all the deities, Aesir and Vanir alike. He was so wise that he could answer any question that was put to him. He was constantly journeying through the world to teach his wisdom to others, and it happened that one night he came to the home of some dwarfs. These dwarfs killed Kvasir and mixed his blood with honey. From this they brewed a mead that gave the gift of poetry to any who tasted it.

Not long after, the dwarfs killed a giant couple. Their son, Suttung, came to seek vengeance, but the dwarfs saved themselves by offering him their precious mead. Suttung took the mead of poetry and hid it in a secret place inside a mountain, setting his daughter Gunnlod (GUN-luhth) to guard it.

Odin heard about the marvelous mead and determined to obtain it for the Aesir. Calling himself Bolverk, he set off to see the giant Baugi, Suttung's brother. On the way he came upon nine of Baugi's workers mowing hay, and he caused them to kill one another with their scythes. When Odin reached Baugi's hall, the giant confided that things were not going well for him. Because his laborers were all dead, he had no way to get his crops in. Odin offered to work for Baugi in return for a sip of Suttung's mead, and the desperate giant agreed. All summer Odin did the work of nine men, and when winter arrived he and Baugi went to Suttung to ask for payment.

Suttung refused, so Baugi and Odin decided to trick him. Odin gave Baugi an auger and had him drill a hole into the mountainside. Then Odin turned himself into a snake. He slithered through the hole to the secret hiding place, where lonely Gunnlod welcomed him. After he spent three nights with her, she granted him three sips of the mead. With those three sips, Odin drank up every last drop. Then he turned himself into an eagle and flew away as quickly as he could.

Suttung saw Odin take flight. He likewise became an eagle and flew after the god. When the Aesir sighted Odin approaching Asgard, hotly pursued, they quickly set jars out in the courtyard. Odin spat the mead into the jars. Ever afterward the jars of mead were kept by the Aesir as a great treasure. There were some men and women, however, whom the Aesir favored with an occasional taste of the mead. These people became great poets, and they called poetry the gift of Odin.

and the household. She knew the fates of all beings but kept this knowledge to herself. She was served by several other goddesses, among them Fulla, who looked after Frigg's belongings and shared her secrets; Syn, who guarded the door of Frigg's hall; Hlin (HLEEN), who protected those whom Frigg wished to keep safe; and Gna, Frigg's messenger and errand runner.

midgards Ormurin

The Thunderer

The most popular and beloved of all the Vikings' deities was Thor; farmers and seafarers were especially devoted to him. The son of Odin and the Earth, he was the god of weather and the protector of humankind. He rode through the heavens in a chariot pulled by two goats, brandishing his great hammer to make the thunder and bring rain for the crops. With this hammer he also fought the giants who were the enemies of Asgard and Midgard.

Thor was famous for his unkempt red beard, his great strength, his huge appetite, his straightforwardness, his quick temper, and his kindly heart. He had two devoted servants, a boy and a girl named Thjalfi (THYAWL-fee) and Roskva, who accompanied him on his many travels among humans and giants. Thor sometimes had relationships with giant women, but he remained devoted to his wife, Sif. She had the gift of prophecy and watched over the growing grain, which ripened to the same color as her golden hair.

The Warrior and the Wolf

The bravest of the gods was Tyr (TEER), whom warriors prayed to. He had only one hand, and this was because of a prophecy that a huge wolf named Fenrir would someday cause great harm to the gods. To trick Fenrir, Odin had had the dwarfs make a magical fetter, which looked like a thin silk ribbon but was stronger than an iron chain. Fenrir

One of Thor's greatest enemies was the Midgard Serpent, who encircled the world and caused storms at sea. Thor once went fishing for the Serpent, using an ox head as bait. He hooked the monster and, using all his divine strength, hauled it aboard his boat. Unfortunately a giant who had come along on the fishing trip lost his nerve and cut the line. The Midgard Serpent slipped back into the sea before Thor could strike it with his hammer.

would not let the gods put the ribbon around him unless they pledged that they would set him loose afterward. As a sign of that pledge, he demanded that one of the gods put a hand in his mouth. Tyr did so, and the gods bound Fenrir. The more the wolf struggled, the tighter the fetter became, and he bit off Tyr's hand. But Tyr's sacrifice ensured that Fenrir would remain bound and harmless until the end of time.

Odin's Other Children

Many more deities belonged to the family of the Aesir. Heimdall (HAYM-duhl), the watchman of the gods, guarded the rainbow bridge that led into Asgard. The son of nine sisters, he could see a hundred miles into the distance, day or night, and could hear the sound of wool growing on a sheep. The goddess Idun (EE-thun) was the keeper of the magical apples that the deities ate to remain young; her husband was Bragi, the god of poetry. Baldr, a son of Frigg and Odin, was handsome, wise, sweet-spoken, and merciful. When he gave a judgment there was nothing that could change it. His wife was Nanna. Their son Forseti was able to solve any legal dispute.

The goddess Var witnessed all promises made between men and women, and punished those who broke their vows. Ull was a great archer, skier, and warrior. Sol drove the chariot of the sun, and her brother Mani drove the chariot of the moon. Eir was the goddess of healing. Saga was the storyteller of the Aesir; every day Odin visited her hall and they drank together from golden cups. The goddess Sjofn (SYUHFN) turned people's minds to love.

Tyr was one of Scandinavia's most ancient deities. This sixth-century Swedish die, used for making helmet plates, is believed to depict the warrior god chaining up the monstrous wolf Fenrir.

Bringers of Pleasure and Plenty

The first war in the world was between the Aesir and the Vanir, a family of deities concerned with wealth and fertility. The war happened on account of the Vanir sorceress Gollveig ("Gold-might"), who visited Asgard and somehow aroused the anger of Odin and his sons. They tried to kill her, first with spears and then with fire. Three times they tried to burn her, and yet she lived. When the other Vanir learned how Gollveig had been mistreated, they attacked Asgard. After long fighting, the two sides agreed to make peace. To seal their treaty they exchanged hostages, and so Njord (NYORTH) left the Vanir to join the Aesir, remaining with them until the end of the world.

Njord was a god of ships and the sea; his home in Asgard was named Shipyard. He could control the wind, calm the waves, and put out fire. All the wealth of the ocean belonged to Njord. People prayed to him for good sailing and fishing and for prosperity in general. For a time he was married to Skadi (SKAH-thee), called the snowshoe goddess, who was a skier, archer, and hunter. But Skadi wanted to live in the mountains and Njord wished to remain by the sea, so they went their separate ways.

The Divine Twins

Njord had two children, Frey ("Lord") and Freyja (FRAY-juh; "Lady"). Both were very beautiful and extremely powerful. Their gifts to humankind were the pleasures of love and the bounty of the earth.

Frey was responsible for the fertility of humans, animals, and the land. He ruled over the light elves, the spirits that helped plants grow. His wife was Gerd (GERTH), from the giants' realm in the north; when she raised her arms, light shimmered over the sea and sky.

People prayed to Frey for peace and plenty, and made offerings to him when they married. Feasts were held in his honor in springtime. To the Swedes, who regarded him as their divine ancestor, Frey was God of the World.

The greatest of all the goddesses was Freyja. She rode into battle with the Valkyries and chose half of the dead warriors to go to her hall Folkvangar. She was master of a form of magic called *seidr* (SAYTHR), which she taught to Odin. Volvas, women who practiced divination, looked to her for power and support. Freyja was also a goddess of fertility and love. People prayed to her for children and for help in their love lives, and they often composed love songs in her honor.

Freyja drove a cart pulled by two cats. She could also travel in the form of a falcon by putting on her falcon cloak. She made many journeys in search of her wandering husband, Od (OHTH), weeping tears of red gold when she did not find him. They had a daughter named Hnoss ("Treasure"). The Disir (DEE-sir), female guardian spirits or ancestors, were Freyja's followers.

The Troublemaker of the Gods

There was one god in Asgard who came from neither the Aesir nor the Vanir but was actually the son of giants. His name was Loki (LOH-kee). Handsome, clever, amusing, and unpredictable, he was a favorite traveling companion of both Odin and Thor. However, his practical jokes and bad judgment often placed the other deities in difficult situations. Fortunately, his trickery usually solved the problems he caused.

Loki had the power to change into various animals. Once, when he was in the shape of a mare, he gave birth to the eight-legged stallion Sleipnir (SLAYP-nir). Sleipnir became Odin's horse, faithfully carrying him to all the worlds. But Loki had three other children, mothered by the giant woman Angrboda

Odin upon his eight-legged horse, Sleipnir, from a Gotland picture stone. The woman in front of Odin may be his wife, Frigg, or a Valkyrie.

45

THE TREASURES OF THE GODS

Once, as a practical joke, Loki cut off all of Sif's beautiful long blond hair. Thor was furious at this treatment of his wife and threatened to break every bone in the trickster's body. But Loki promised that he would make up for his prank by having the dwarfs forge new hair out of gold for Sif.

With his usual cunning, Loki got the dwarfs to make not only Sif's golden hair but also a spear and a heavy gold arm ring for Odin, a ship and a golden boar for Frey, and a hammer for Thor. All of these were wonderful. As soon as Sif put the golden hair on her head, it began to grow like natural hair. Odin's spear never missed its target, and the arm ring made eight copies of itself every nine nights. Frey's ship was large enough for all the Aesir to travel in together; no matter where it was going, a fair wind always filled the sail. When the ship was not being used, Frey could fold it up like a piece of cloth and put it in a pouch. Frey's boar could carry a rider through the air or over the water faster than any horse could run, and for nighttime travel its bristles glowed with brilliant light.

But the Aesir judged that Thor's hammer was the best treasure of all. It was unbreakable and could hit anything, no matter how hard. When Thor hurled it at something, it would always return to his hand. He could even make it small enough to carry inside his shirt. It was just the thing for defending Asgard and Midgard from the frost giants. And so this time Loki's trickery resulted in great good fortune for the Aesir.

(ANGR-boh-thuh), who were predicted to do great harm to the gods. First was the wolf Fenrir. Second was the Midgard Serpent. Odin threw the Serpent into the ocean, where it grew so large that it encircled the earth. Third was Hel, who was half black and half white. Odin sent her to rule Niflheim and commanded her to share her provisions with all men who died of illness or old age.

Although Loki was at first welcomed among the gods, his tricks gradually became more and more mean-spirited. The final outrage came when he caused the death of Frigg and Odin's beloved son Baldr. Hel said that she would release Baldr from Niflheim and allow him to return to Asgard only if all of creation mourned him. The Aesir sent swift messengers through the worlds, asking everyone and everything to weep for Baldr. Humans, animals, stones, trees, and even metals cried. But one old giant woman, who was really Loki in disguise, refused to mourn, and so Baldr had to remain among the dead. After that the gods seized Loki, bound him tightly, and imprisoned him in a cave, where he remained until the end of the world.

The Doom of the Gods

It was foretold that the time would come when all creation would be destroyed. This was the Ragnarok (RAG-nuh-ruhk), the Doom of the Gods. First there would be three winters when the whole world would be at war, followed by three exceedingly harsh winters with no summers between them. Then the sun and the moon would be swallowed by wolves, and Fenrir and Loki would break free from their bonds. The Midgard Serpent would come ashore, causing tidal waves as it lashed about, and spew poison over sea and sky. The fiery giant Surt would lead an army out of Muspell, while Loki and Hel would be at the head of the frost giants.

Heimdall would sound his horn to summon the gods to battle. Odin would be the first to ride out from Asgard, accompanied by all the great warriors he had gathered in Valhalla. Thor and Frey would be close behind. Fenrir would swallow Odin, but the All-father's son Vidar (VEE-thar) would kill the wolf. Thor would destroy the Midgard Serpent, only to die of its poison moments afterward. Heimdall and Loki would kill each other, as would Tyr and the hound of Hel. Frey would be killed by Surt, who would then burn up the whole world.

Yet this would not be the end of everything. A new, green earth would rise up out of the sea, and the sun's daughter would take her mother's place in the sky. Two sons of Odin and two sons of Thor would survive, and Baldr would return from the dead to join them. Where Asgard once stood they would have a new divine realm on Idavoll (EE-thuh-vuhl), "the plain that renews itself." And from a hidden wood there would come a woman and a man to be the parents of a new human race.

This fragment of a stone cross found on the Isle of Man shows Odin, with one of his ravens still on his shoulder, being devoured by Fenrir at the Ragnarok, or Doom of the Gods.

CHAPTER FOUR

A WORLD OF HONOR AND LOYALTY

CATTLE DIE, KINDRED DIE,
   EVERY MAN IS MORTAL:
BUT THE GOOD NAME NEVER DIES
   OF ONE WHO HAS DONE WELL.

CATTLE DIE, KINDRED DIE,
   EVERY MAN IS MORTAL:
BUT I KNOW ONE THING THAT NEVER DIES,
   THE GLORY OF THE GREAT DEAD.

These lines from the Viking Age poem *Havamal* (HAH-vuh-mahl), "The Words of the High One," express beliefs that were at the heart of Viking society. Death was certain and always potentially near at hand. How and when death came, as well as the circumstances and events of life, were not under a person's control; the power of fate ruled all such things. But a person could control how she or he faced the decrees of fate, and this was where honor came in. A person who made the most—or at least the best—of life's ups and downs would be well remembered by generations to come.

Havamal, or *The Words of the High One,* is the longest of all the Old Norse poems that have come down to us. It seems to have begun as a collection of the wise sayings of Odin (the High One). Over time more wise sayings and bits of advice were added to it, along with the stories of Odin's winning the mead of poetry and the knowledge of the runes. Reading *Havamal* today can give us a good picture of many of the ideals and concerns of Viking Age men.

Some of the High One's advice is very practical: Get up early if you have things to do, whether you're planning a raid or simply have a lot of farmwork. Keep your wits about you when you travel, and don't leave home without your weapons, because you never know when you might run into trouble. Drink only in moderation—if you get drunk, you may act like a fool and not even remember it the next day. Don't keep yourself awake all night worrying; you'll just be tired the next day, and your problems will be as bad as ever.

The *Havamal* has a great deal of advice about the proper behavior of hosts and guests: A host should give a newly arrived guest a hearty welcome, a place by the fire, water to wash with, clean clothing, and food and drink. A host should also listen attentively to whatever a guest has to say. A guest should not taunt or quarrel with other guests, should not eat or drink too much, and, above all, should not overstay his welcome. A guest also needs to look out for his own interests: He should not arrive at a feast too early (the food and drink might not be ready) or too late (the good stuff might be all gone).

The High One has much to say about friendship, too: Be loyal to your friends, and to their friends; never offer friendship to your friends' enemies. Visit your friends often, and exchange gifts with them. Share your true thoughts and feelings with your friends. Never be the one to end a friendship. Without friends, life is not worth living.

As for wealth, it's only worth having if you share it with friends—after all, enemies could come and take it away in an instant. And while it's always better to be alive than to be a corpse, it's better to be dead than to be a coward. In the words of the *Havamal,* "the generous and bold have the best lives."

To live honorably meant to be loyal to family, friends, comrades, and leaders; to keep all vows or promises; to be hospitable to guests; to give generous presents; and to avenge injustice. Glorious deeds, such as participation in Viking expeditions, and good deeds, such as building causeways to help travelers, added greatly to a person's reputation. So did skills and talents, and qualities such as eloquence, cleverness, and self-control. Bravery in danger, even in the face of unbeatable odds, and steadfastness in all situations were the most praiseworthy qualities of all, and the most essential to honor.

◄ *A Viking Age burial ground in Sweden. It was of great importance to the Vikings to live in such a way that they would be well remembered after death.*

Law and Order

Another important ingredient of honor was respect for the law. In fact, one of the consequences of breaking the law was loss of honor. For this and other reasons, Viking Age Scandinavians tended to be very law-abiding, if not when they were out raiding, at least at home in their own districts. And wherever they settled overseas, from Greenland to England, they established this same respect for the law.

Laws dealt with nearly all aspects of society, including property, inheritance, marriage, divorce, slavery, hunting rights, livestock, magic, trade, and the treatment of foreigners. Of course, Scandinavian law was also very much concerned with crime.To steal something from a locked building was the most serious kind of theft. Many degrees of homicide were recognized, from accidental killing, killing in self-defense, and killing in a fair fight, to the far graver offenses of killing in a holy place, killing someone but refusing to admit to it, murder by arson, and premeditated murder.

For the worst crimes the penalty was death. Mutilation and flogging (whipping) were also sometimes used as punishments. Troublesome law breakers were often outlawed, either permanently or for a fixed amount of time. As an outlaw a person was banished from a particular region or country. If the outlaw remained in, or returned to, the forbidden territory, anyone there had the legal right to kill him or her.

Many homicides were punished by a fine called wergild, which was set according to the rank of the person killed. In the Danelaw, for example, a free farmer's wergild was eight half-marks of gold. Wergild usually took the form of a certain amount of precious metal, but it might also be counted out in cattle or woolens. The fine was paid to the family of the slain by the killer and his or her family. The victim of an assault also received wergild, paid by the person who had injured him or her.

Law enforcement in the Viking world was the responsibility of the individuals involved; there was no police force. For this reason people sometimes felt that legal procedures failed to provide justice—for example, a killer could refuse to pay wergild. In such a case the dead person's family might avenge the killing by slaying a member of the killer's family. Old Icelandic literature is full of feuds that started in this way. Fortunately, such happenings were rare. Most Viking Age Scandinavians felt well served and protected by the law, and were happy to support it.

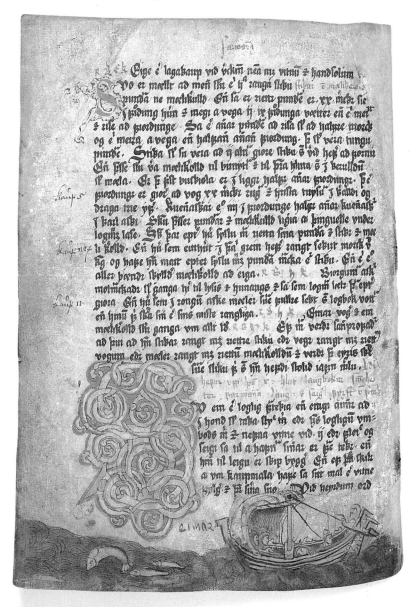

The Viking settlers of Iceland established a law code early on. Until 1280 the laws were passed on orally; then they were written down in the Jonsbok. *This page from a sixteenth-century Icelandic manuscript of the* Jonsbok *records laws about shipping freight.*

Government by the People

Laws were made and legal cases were judged at local and regional assemblies called Things. These met for a week or two at least once a year, often around the time of the summer solstice. All free men had the right to attend the Things and to speak out at them. They sat on juries to hear and settle disputes. They debated laws and politics and considered issues as important as selecting or

A meeting of Iceland's Althing, with the lawspeaker presiding from the rock in the center of the picture. This reconstruction was painted by English artist W. G. Collingwood, who researched the painting's details on a trip to Iceland in the 1870s.

approving a new king and choosing the country's official religion. All decisions had to be agreed to by the assembly of free men, who gave their approval by shouting and brandishing their weapons.

The larger Things have been called "part legislative session and part country fair." Men might travel great distances to attend, bringing their whole families. They set up tents around the Thing site, which was always outdoors. Along with the legal proceedings, there were markets, probably religious ceremonies, and plenty of opportunities for socializing.

Scandinavian colonists took the institution of the Thing with them to their new homes abroad. The most famous Thing, and the one we have the most information about, was Iceland's Althing, the national assembly. It was presided over by a man known as the lawspeaker. He was elected by the island's leading landowners, the *godar* (GOH-thar), for a three-year term. Each year at the Althing the lawspeaker publicly recited one-third of the law code, which he had committed to memory. As an authority on the law, he had great influence; all real power, however, remained in the hands of the *godar.*

The authority of the great assembly of free men varied from region to region and at different times during the Viking Age. In the Scandinavian homelands, the power of the Things tended to decrease as the power of kings increased from the tenth century on. Many rulers turned the Things, especially the large regional ones, to their own use, treating them as advisory bodies. Kings also employed the Things to help present their policies to the people. And although the Things gave a voice to all free men, the voices of the wealthy and powerful were nearly always heard loudest.

The Three Classes

Among the Vikings people belonged to one of three social classes: the unfree, the free, and the rulers. According to the Viking Age poem *Rigsthula* (REEGS-thoo-luh), these classes had a divine origin. Long ago, the god Heimdall had disguised himself as a man named Rig and traveled the earth. He spent three nights with three different couples, Great-Grandfather and Great-Grandmother, Grandfather and Grandmother, and Father and Mother. Nine months after Rig's visit, each of the women gave birth to a son. Great-Grandmother's son was named Thrall ("Slave"); he was the ancestor of all the unfree. Grandmother's boy was called Karl ("Farmer"), and his descendants made up the free class. Mother's child was Jarl ("Noble"); all rulers were descended from him.

The Unfree

As in many cultures of the past, slavery played a large role in the economy of the Vikings. There was a great demand for slaves in the wealthy Byzantine and Muslim empires; as both raiders and traders, the Vikings

VIKING SOCIETY IN THE AFTERLIFE

In the native Scandinavian religion there were differing beliefs about the afterlife. Since people were buried with belongings and provisions, it seems that life after death was considered very similar to life before death. Many people believed that a dead person's spirit stayed in the grave, sometimes coming out to wander around his or her old home. But there was also a strong belief that the dead spent the afterlife in different divine realms. Where people went depended less on what they had done during their lives than on who they had been.

Free men and nobles who were killed in battle went either to the goddess Freyja's hall or to Odin's Valhalla. In Valhalla they practiced their fighting skills during the day and feasted with Odin at night. Men who died from other causes went to Niflheim, the rather dark and unpleasant world ruled by the goddess Hel. Hel also had a hall full of poisonous snakes and other tortures for men who had committed the most serious crimes. Women who died unmarried spent the afterlife with the goddess Gefjon (GEF-yuhn). Married women went to Freyja. Slaves of both sexes, and perhaps also common farmers, went to Thor. And so the social classes and the roles of men and women remained as distinct in death as in life.

were well equipped to meet this demand. The slave trade quickly became one of their most profitable enterprises.

Most of the slaves the Vikings sold were people they had captured on slave hunts in the Slavic lands of eastern Europe or on raids in the British Isles and other areas. They also bought many slaves at markets to sell them again elsewhere. Other slaves were prisoners of war, criminals sentenced to slavery, people who could not pay their debts, or children of slaves.

Slaves were not only a major part of the Vikings' foreign trade, but were also important to their lifestyle at home. All but the smallest farms had at least a few slaves to do heavy and dirty chores such as hauling firewood, fertilizing the fields with manure, and feeding the pigs. Female slaves helped with the housework: They might grind grain, press and pleat cloth (using a glass ball as an iron and a whalebone plaque as an ironing board), cook and serve meals, and prepare flax and wool for spinning.

Slaves had few rights and no legal protections. They could not bear arms or be heard at the Thing. They were bought and sold like farm animals. If they ran away, they were likely to be hunted down and killed. Female slaves were frequently expected to have relationships with their masters, whether they wanted to or not. And when an owner died, a slave was often executed to accompany him or her in death. Sometimes, out of loyalty or for other reasons, a slave actually volunteered for this fate.

The life of a slave was not always unbearable. For one thing, the mistreatment of slaves was a stain on an owner's reputation. Especially skilled, beautiful, or loyal slaves might live quite comfortably and be treated with much respect. Eventually, they might even be freed as a reward for faithful service. Slaves were allowed to marry, but their children were automatically slaves, too. Sometimes slaves could earn their own money, which they could use to buy their freedom; it was also possible for some other person to buy a slave's freedom for him or her.

The Free

Most Viking Age Scandinavians belonged to the free class, which included everyone from peddlers and poor farm laborers to celebrated skalds and wealthy landowners. No matter how rich or poor, all free men had certain rights, which they were very proud and protective of—and with good reason, for nowhere else in medieval Europe did the common people have such privileges and respect.

Most Viking freemen provided for their families by farming, hunting, and fishing. This illustration from a medieval Icelandic manuscript shows the result of a successful fishing trip. Fish and whale meat could be eaten fresh, or dried and salted to store for later use.

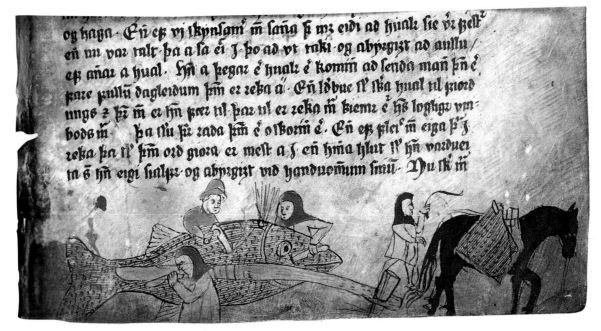

Along with the right to participate in the Thing, free men had the right to bear weapons and enjoyed full legal protection. It was they who were called on to fight in their country's defense, to make laws, and to pass judgments. They grew crops, raised livestock, crafted tools and weapons, produced artwork, and composed poetry. They were the backbone of Viking society.

The typical free man was a farmer who owned and worked his own land. At the same time he might also be a hunter, fisherman, sailor, trader, or warrior. He could belong to a fellowship, which might be a religious society, a band of warriors sworn to the same leader, or a group of men who owned a ship together. He might even go off on a summer-long raiding expedition. But no matter what else he did or how much he was away from his farm, he always cherished his ties with his land.

Free men who did not have land had what was called land hunger—the intense desire for land of their own. This desire drove many to leave home permanently and settle in the Viking colonies. Some landless free men, along with others who already owned land but were eager to increase their holdings, went out in search of wealth as raiders, merchants, or professional warriors. Since the combination of wealth and heroic deeds was greatly respected in Scandinavia, a man who returned home from a successful Viking expedition could not only buy land but might well become quite influential in his community.

The Rulers

The most prominent man in a district was generally the wealthiest, with large land holdings that had been in his family for many generations. Such men made up the ruling class in Viking society; they were the jarls (YARLS), the nobles or chieftains. They might be quite powerful, with control over large regions. Some were completely independent rulers, like the jarls of Trondheim in western Norway. Other jarls were subject to the authority of kings, who gave them responsibility for particular districts.

King was a very flexible term in the Viking Age. Early on it was used for any chieftain who was able to maintain a loyal following of warriors. To attract the right sort of men, he had to have a reputation for leadership, bravery, good faith, and generosity. To keep warriors in his service he also had to be wealthy enough to feed, arm, entertain, and reward them well.

A king's fame and income were assured by control of the waterways—the roads to plunder, conquest, and trade. His power was also based on the fact that he was usually the largest landowner in the region he ruled. He had to be a descendant of kings, on either his mother's or his father's side. To add to his prestige, he might even trace his ancestry back to Odin, Frey, or a legendary hero. His authority was upheld by the approval and support of the free men and nobles of his kingdom.

For much of the Viking Age the Scandinavian countries were divided into many kingdoms. Even within these the various regions remained quite independent, cherishing their own laws and customs. But gradually royal power increased, and the number of separate kingdoms decreased. This was partly because individual kings were ambitious to expand their influence. More importantly, the free class was often glad to see large territories united under a single strong ruler, for unification tended to encourage more peaceful and prosperous conditions.

The king's major responsibilities were to defend and enrich his kingdom. He organized the building of fortresses and other defenses, and personally led his army in battle. He was concerned with promoting trade, guaranteeing protection for the trade routes and merchants in his realm. Another important role of the king was to guard his country's interests in treaties and other agreements with foreign nations. Finally, the king was very often a religious leader: If he followed the native religion, he prayed and sacrificed to the gods on his people's behalf. If he was a Christian, he encouraged his people to convert to Christianity, too—sometimes using threats and violence to make his point.

A wealthy woman of the Viking Age may have looked something like the goddess depicted by this silver and gold pendant from sixth-century Sweden. She wears a large necklace, and her long hair is knotted at the back of her head. Carrying herself with dignity, she is obviously held in high esteem.

Women in the Viking Age

While a man was born into his class, a woman's class depended on that of her husband (although normally this would be the same as her parents' class). Women could not rule, and there is no evidence that they could express their opinions at the Thing. But this does not necessarily mean that women had an inferior position; in fact, their contributions to society were highly valued. What's more, Viking women had many rights that were not enjoyed by women in the rest of Europe, including the right to divorce on demand and the rights to own and inherit property.

IF YOU LIVED IN VIKING AGE SCANDINAVIA

If you had been born in Scandinavia during the Viking Age, your way of life would have been determined by the facts of your birth—whether you were a girl or a boy, free or slave, wealthy or poor. With this chart you can trace the course your life might have taken as the child of a free farmer.

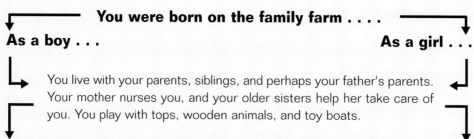

You were born on the family farm . . . .

As a boy . . .   **As a girl . . .**

You live with your parents, siblings, and perhaps your father's parents. Your mother nurses you, and your older sisters help her take care of you. You play with tops, wooden animals, and toy boats.

As soon as you are old enough you begin to help your father with the farmwork. Your father teaches you how to make and repair tools and other items used by your family. You also learn to fish, hunt, and fight.

▼

As a teenager you may become a warrior and go on a Viking expedition or fight in the king's army, especially if you are a younger son. Otherwise you continue to work on the family farm.

▼

In your twenties you probably get married. If you are the oldest son, you stay on the family farm, which you will inherit. Otherwise you buy or rent a farm of your own. You spend most of your time doing farmwork, fishing, hunting, and making the things your family needs. You relax by playing board games, telling and listening to stories, and visiting with friends. You may join a fellowship, and now and then you may go away on a Viking expedition. You fight in the king's army whenever necessary and attend the local Thing every year. You teach your sons everything they will need to know as adults.

As soon as you are old enough you begin to help your mother with the housework. You go with her to gather berries and to milk the farm's cows and goats. She teaches you to spin, weave, sew, dye wool, grind grain, cook, and make cheese.

▼

As a teenager you are old enough to be married. Your parents choose your husband, but only with your consent. They give you a dowry, which will remain your personal property throughout your marriage. You may divorce your husband at any time for any reason.

▼

As a housewife you have much responsibility and are greatly respected. You make all of your family's clothes and prepare all of its food. You also preserve food and store it for the winter. You relax by playing board games, telling and listening to stories, and visiting with friends. When your husband is away at war, on a hunting trip, or on a voyage, you protect and run the entire farm. You teach your daughters everything they will need to know as adults.

As a senior citizen you are respected for your wisdom and experience. When you die your body is either cremated or buried. Your remains may be buried with many of your belongings. Your family or friends may have a rune stone raised to your memory.

Viking women were just as likely to be literate as Viking men; we know definitely of one woman who was a rune carver and another who was a skald. There were probably quite a few women artisans. Rune stones tell of women who sponsored the building of causeways and jetties for the loading and unloading of ships. Women also had important roles in the native Scandinavian religion, especially in the worship of Frigg, Freyja, and the Disir, the goddesses and spirits who watched over farm and family.

The Honorable Housewife

The average Viking woman lived on a farm with her husband and children. Marriage was an equal partnership. Husband and wife each had their own distinct roles on the farm, but both were absolutely necessary to the family's survival.

A wife was responsible for all household matters. She nourished her family with porridges, stews, flatbreads, and cheese. She kept the house clean and tidy. She washed clothes and mended them when necessary. She spent a great deal of time spinning and weaving, then sewed the finished cloth into garments for the family. At harvest time she joined her husband in the fields with her sickle to help bring in the grain and hay.

The Viking housewife had a very dignified position, symbolized by the bunch of keys she wore at her waist. These were for the locks of the house and all the farm buildings, which she alone was responsible for. If her husband went away on a trading or raiding expedition, she took on the complete responsibility of running and protecting the farm.

Some women did not stay at home but took part in their menfolks' adventures. Many warriors of the Great Army that invaded England in the ninth century were accompanied by their wives and children. Women also traveled with the Rus merchants in eastern Europe; most of these women were slaves, but some of them were probably wives, and a few may have been merchants themselves. A great many Scandinavian women braved considerable dangers and hardships to settle in the colonies overseas. Courageous, steadfast, and devoted to their families, such women truly lived up to the Viking ideal of honor.

CHAPTER FIVE

IN THE WAKE OF THE LONGSHIPS

The Viking Age lasted for nearly three centuries, from 793 to 1066. During this time Scandinavians played a greater role in the world community than at any other time in history. Today it can be difficult to find traces of the Vikings' legacy in some of the areas where they were active—in Russia, for example. But there is no doubt that the Vikings changed the course of history in Europe—and they, in turn, were changed by their contacts with the world outside Scandinavia.

The ruins of a large Viking farmstead in the Shetland Islands. Northern Scotland, including the Shetlands, remained closely tied to Norway for centuries after the end of the Viking Age.

Lasting Impressions

The Vikings' impact on Europe was both direct and indirect. They supplied luxury goods such as furs and walrus ivory to the upper classes, and their trading activities added to the continent's general prosperity. On the other hand, Viking raids prompted many coastal communities to move inland to be safer from attack by

sea. A number of monasteries and trading centers were abandoned. Rulers built coastal forts and fortified bridges against the Northmen, but nevertheless there were areas where European society was seriously disrupted by Viking invasions.

This was particularly true in Frankia, where the organization of both the government and the Catholic Church almost completely broke down. Powerful landowners took advantage of the situation and set themselves up as lords of their localities. Less powerful men offered their services to these lords in return for protection. This was the beginning of French feudalism, a form of social organization and government that would spread throughout Europe and prevail until the end of the Middle Ages. It was adopted at least partly in response to the violence of the Northmen.

Britain's Scandinavian Inheritance

Of all the foreign lands where the Vikings plundered and settled, their activities had the greatest impact on the British Isles. Some of the effects were short-lived, such as Scandinavian influence on English art styles during the tenth and eleventh centuries. Other effects of the Viking invasions have lasted to the present. For instance, many of the fortresses that Alfred the Great built in defense against the Northmen developed into towns that still exist.

Modern English contains over six hundred words that come from Old Norse. Some, such as *berserk,* are used infrequently, while at least one is used on a weekly basis: *Thursday* means "Thor's Day." Here are some more of the words that the Vikings contributed to our language.

Animals	birth	loose
bull	booth	low
kid	dirt	odd
narwhal	egg	rotten
reindeer	gap	sly
walrus	law	ugly
	race	weak
People	sky	wrong
fellow	steak	
husband	trust	
sister	window	Verbs
		call
Parts of the Body		cast
calf	Pronouns	crawl
leg	both	cut
skin	their	die
skull	them	droop
	they	drown
		glitter
Parts of Ships		lift
keel	Adjectives	scare
starboard	angry	take
stern	awkward	thrust
	flat	want
Other Nouns	hungry	
axle	ill	

And because of the Viking settlements in the Danelaw, more than six hundred Old Norse words are part of the modern English language.

Even though the Viking Age came to its "official" end in 1066, many Scandinavians in the British Isles continued to have strong ties to their homeland. This was especially true in the Orkney and Shetland Islands, north of Scotland. Both groups of islands were governed by Norway until the middle of the fifteenth century. In the Orkneys the people even spoke a variant of Norwegian until the nineteenth century.

A large number of place names in the British Isles were given by the Vikings and remain in use today. In the Danelaw the most common Scandinavian place names were based on the Old Norse words *by* ("village") and *thorp* ("farmstead"); examples are Danby ("Dane Town") and Hackenthorpe ("Hakon's Farm"). Other names used such words as *dalr* ("valley"), *ness* ("headland"), *vik* ("bay"), *ey* ("island"), and *fjordr* ("inlet"). So we have, for example, the towns of Scorradale and Westness (in the Orkneys), Lerwick (the capital of the Shetlands), Anglesey (off the coast of Wales), and Waterford (in Ireland).

Before the Vikings arrived, Ireland was a completely rural country with many local kings constantly warring against one another. The Northmen established Ireland's first towns—Dublin, Wexford, Waterford, Limerick, and others—and these are still among the island's main urban centers. Along with the towns came trade and money, which were also completely new to the Irish. The modern Irish words for *market* and *penny*, for example, come from Old Norse; the Irish language had no words for such concepts. Finally, the Viking presence in their island spurred the Irish kingdoms to begin overcoming their differences and move toward uniting their country under a single king.

The Vikings brought their ideas about government and law to many parts of the British Isles. Today the Isle of Man's parliament is still called the Tynwald, from the Old Norse *thingvollr,* "assembly plain." Just as in Viking times, it meets outdoors on Tynwald Hill every July 5 to publicly ratify the laws that have been passed during the foregoing year. In England, the Danelaw received its name because in that region Danish law held sway. A late-tenth-century legal code from the Danelaw decreed that courts should be made up of twelve of the community's leading men,

The opening ceremony of the Isle of Man's parliament takes place on Tynwald Hill, where the island's Thing met in Viking times.

who were required to swear that they would judge all cases fairly and impartially. This court was the ancestor of the modern twelve-person sworn jury.

Change at Home

The foundations of modern Scandinavia were laid during the Viking Age. This period saw the birth of a true national consciousness in each of the Scandinavian countries. People began to think of themselves not just as citizens of the Trondheim region, for example, but as citizens of Norway. Under strong kings, the many small Scandinavian kingdoms were gradually joined together. By the end of the eleventh century Denmark and Norway were nation-states unified under a single ruler. The same process was well under way in Sweden, to be completed in the twelfth century.

Another of the great happenings of the Viking Age was the beginning of urban life in Scandinavia. Many towns came into being and with them flourishing trade, greater specialization in crafts than before, and many other innovations. For instance, Viking merchants traditionally sold their goods for a certain amount of silver, which they weighed out with portable scales. Trade contact with England, Frankia, the Byzantine Empire, and the Arab world introduced the use of money. Soon Scandinavian kings were having their own coins minted, which helped them to control trade and at the same time proclaimed their power. By the end of the eleventh century money was a common form of payment in the Scandinavian countries.

This horn full of silver coins, jewelry, and other valuables was buried with a Viking man.

The New Religion

Viking raiders, traders, and settlers all came into contact with Christianity, the dominant religion of Europe. In the ninth century the church began to send missionaries to Scandinavia. The new faith made gradual inroads, often peacefully coexisting with the native religion. Many people came to Christianity out of sincere belief in its teachings. Many others seem to have accepted it primarily for its usefulness. Some Vikings were even baptized repeatedly just so that they could get the outfits of white clothing and other gifts that were given to new Christians.

Scandinavian merchants quickly recognized that they would have better trading relations with Christians if they adopted at least some aspects of their religion; Christians preferred to do business with other Christians. Scandinavian kings found that the same was true in international relations: Those who converted to Christianity were able to negotiate much more favorable agreements with the Christian kings of Europe. The Viking monarchs also realized that the strong power structure of the Catholic Church could support their rule and help them extend their authority.

And so the Scandinavian kings led the way in converting to the new religion. But Christianity was not always embraced willingly or peacefully. For instance, Olaf Haraldsson (later Saint Olaf), who ruled Norway from 1015 to 1030, ordered chieftains who did not accept Christianity to be blinded, maimed, or outlawed. To the free class Olaf offered the choice of being killed,

This fourteenth-century painting shows King Olaf Haraldsson, who made Christianity the official religion of Norway, surrounded by scenes of his death in battle.

leaving the country, or being baptized. By the eleventh century Norway and Denmark were officially Christian, and Sweden followed in the next century. Nevertheless, the old ways died hard, and some ancient beliefs and practices lingered in the countryside for a long time.

The Continuing Story

During the Viking Age Scandinavia absorbed many influences from other countries, and conversion to Christianity brought the region into the mainstream of European culture. Yet the break with the past was not complete. Even well into the twentieth century, rural Scandinavian families lived very much as their Viking ancestors did. Fishing boats were built with the same techniques that had been used in the construction of the great Viking ships, and women wove cloth on upright looms nearly identical to those of their foremothers. The summer solstice, when Viking families once came together at the great Things, is still a time of festivals and community celebrations.

Much of the Viking legacy in Scandinavia is embodied in the words people use every day. A great number of place names from that period have survived to the present. Many Viking Age first names—such as Bjorn, Harald, Olaf, and Rolf for boys; and Sigrid, Ingrid, Gudrun, and Asa for girls—continue to be popular in Scandinavia. And the modern Swedish, Danish, and Norwegian languages are all descended from Old Norse.

The Icelandic Saga

In many ways it is in Iceland that the Viking spirit has survived strongest. The island remained an independent republic until 1262, when it came under Norwegian rule, and in 1380 it passed into Danish control. Nevertheless, the Icelanders were

able to keep the Althing alive as a court until 1800. In 1845 the Althing was reestablished, and on June 17, 1944, Iceland once more became an independent republic. Its capital is Reykjavik (RAY-kyuh-veek), the site of the first Viking settlement, and its parliament is still called the Althing.

Thingvellir National Park in Iceland preserves and honors the place where the republic's national assembly began.

NEW LIFE FOR OLD LEGENDS

The nineteenth century saw a great surge of interest in the old myths and legends of northern Europe. Scholars began to study them; artists, composers, and writers drew inspiration from them. The popular image of the Vikings in their horned helmets comes to us from works of this period.

One of the most famous of these nineteenth-century works is *The Ring of the Nibelungs* (the Ring Cycle), a series of four operas created by the German composer Richard Wagner (REE-kard VAHG-ner). With stirring, dramatic music, the Ring operas present Wagner's version of the stories of Sigurd the dragon slayer and the Doom of the Gods. These operas continue to be performed to enthusiastic audiences all over the world.

In the twentieth century, English scholar and writer J. R. R. Tolkien used elements of the Vikings' mythology, language, literature, and customs to create his own fantasy world. Tolkien's *The Hobbit* and *The Lord of the Rings* transport readers to a place called Middle Earth, where dragons guard vast treasures, dwarfs live under mountains, elves make merry in the woods, warriors fight heroically, and the forces of good and evil battle over an enchanted ring. These novels remain popular with readers of all ages, and they have been made into films, radio programs, and even games.

In the 1960s the Scandinavian god Thor took on new life as a comic book super-hero. In Marvel Comics' *Journeys into Mystery* and *Thor,* the mighty thunder god has come to earth, where he wields his hammer to battle crime in the modern city. In many of his adventures he is joined by other Viking deities and even comes up against his old enemies, the frost giants. Thor has now been featured in more than five hundred comic book issues and a cartoon series—surely one of the most unusual legacies of any culture of the past.

Nearly all Icelanders are directly descended from the island's Viking Age settlers, and they take much pride in the courage and independence of their ancestors. But an even greater source of pride is the Icelandic literary heritage. During the Viking Age Iceland produced numerous skalds, who recited their poems before the kings of Dublin, York, and Norway. After that era came to an end, Icelandic writers of the twelfth and thirteenth centuries brought it back to life in the form of sagas, long tales about historical and legendary heroes. These are among the greatest works of literature produced anywhere in the Middle Ages.

The sagas have been immensely popular ever since they were written. By 1800 all citizens of Iceland could read—and everyone, from poor farmers to wealthy landowners, read the sagas. Family copies were handed down through the generations, treasured as precious heirlooms and proud reminders of the deeds of ancestors. Today Icelanders still read the sagas with enthusiasm—and with ease, for the modern Icelandic language is nearly identical to Old Norse.

There are some forty Icelandic sagas, and nearly all of them tell stories set in the Viking Age. Although based on real people and events (for example, the life of the skald Egill Skallagrimsson), they are what we would call historical novels, combining fact with fiction. They are full of daring expeditions, glorious battles, life-and-death struggles, grand encounters, and courage in the face of incredible odds. The best of them are not only exciting stories but also subtle examinations of human strengths and failings.

If the sagas have a message, it is the old Viking conviction that although fate is inescapable, people can face their destiny in such a way that their honor will long be remembered. "Everyone chooses their own fame," says a character in *Njal's Saga*. As raiders, merchants, settlers, lawmakers, smiths, and poets, the Vikings earned many kinds of fame. Their bravery, creativity, steadfastness, and independent spirit have been remembered for more than a thousand years now, and may well be remembered for a thousand more.

Modern Danes celebrate their Viking heritage at a festival where they dress as their ancestors did and recreate battles and other aspects of Viking society.

The Vikings: A Chronology

793	Viking raiders attack the monastery of Lindisfarne in Northumbria
790s	First Viking raids on Ireland and Scotland
799	First Viking raid on Frankia
841	Norwegian Vikings establish a permanent settlement at Dublin
845	Danish Vikings raid Paris; Frankish king pays the first Danegeld
c. 860	First Rus raid on Constantinople; settlement of Faeroe Islands
c. 862	Rurik becomes first Rus ruler in Novgorod; Rus capital later moved to Kiev
866–874	The Great Army invades and conquers much of England
c. 870	Ingolf Arnarson founds first permanent settlement in Iceland
902–917	King Edward and his sister Aethelflaed reconquer Viking territory in England
911	Foundation of Normandy by Rollo
914–939	Norwegian army conquers and raids in Brittany
930	Foundation of the Althing in Iceland
958–987	Harald Bluetooth rules Denmark, unites it, and makes Christianity the official religion
986	Erik the Red leads the settlement of Greenland; Bjarni Herjolfsson sights North America

995–1000	Olaf Tryggvason rules Norway, temporarily unites it
c. 995–c. 1021	Olaf Skotkonung rules central Sweden, promotes Christianity
c. 1000	Leif Eriksson sails to North America, winters in Vinland; Christianity becomes official religion of Iceland and Greenland
c. 1005–1008	Thorfinn Karlsefni's settlement in Vinland
1013	Danish king Svein Forkbeard invades England
1015–1030	Olaf Haraldsson rules Norway, forces conversion to Christianity
1016–1035	Reign of Knut the Great, first over England and then over Denmark and part of Norway as well
1066	Norwegian king Harald Hardradi invades England, is defeated by Harold Godwinsson; William the Conqueror invades England, defeats Harold, and becomes king

GLOSSARY

Aesir (EYE-sir): the family of deities headed by the god Odin

alliteration: in Viking Age poetry, the repetition of the same consonant or vowel sound two or more times in a line; for example, the repetition of the s sound in "Sun turned from the south, sister of Moon"

archaeologist: a person who studies the remains (such as tools, buildings, and works of art) of past human cultures

Asgard: (AHS-garth): the mythological world where the Aesir lived

Danegeld: a payment made to the Vikings to prevent or stop them from attacking a country or region

Danelaw: the part of eastern and northern England that was settled by the Danes in the ninth century; even after that area was reconquered by the English, Danish law and customs still held sway there.

Disir (DEE-sir): female ancestors or guardian spirits; their leader was the goddess Freyja.

divination: the art of discovering hidden facts about the past, present, or future

dynasty: a line of rulers descended from the same royal ancestor

futhark: the Viking alphabet, consisting of sixteen letters called runes

Germanic: the ethnic group made up of people who spoke languages closely related to modern German

godar (GOH-thar): the nobles of Iceland. They were prominent landowners from important families and also played the chief role in religion and politics.

jarl (yarl): a noble or chieftain

kenning: an expression in which two nouns are combined to describe a thing in a riddle-like way; for example, "spoiler of twigs" was a Viking Age kenning for fire.

manuscript: a book that was written and bound by hand

mead: a drink made from fermented honey

Midgard (MITH-garth)**:** "Middle World" or "Middle Earth"; the world of living human beings

missionary: a person who travels to another place to teach his or her religion to the people of that place

Muspell: the world of fire in Viking mythology

myth: a sacred story; a story that explains or describes the religious beliefs of a people

Niflheim (NIH-fuhl-haym)**:** in Viking mythology, the world of fog, ruled by the goddess Hel; men who did not die in battle went there after death

Norns: three immortal maidens who ruled over fate

personify: to give human characteristics to an idea or thing

Ragnarok (RAG-nuh-ruhk)**:** "the Doom of the Gods"; the destruction of the world by the forces of chaos

runes: the letters of the Viking alphabet

Rus (ROOS)**:** the Scandinavians, mainly from Sweden, who traded, raided, and settled in eastern Europe

saga: a long tale about historical or legendary heroes, written down in medieval Scandinavia or Iceland

skald: a professional poet who composed complex poems and recited them at the courts of kings and nobles

smith: an artist or craftsperson

Thing: an outdoor assembly of free men who gathered to make laws and try legal cases

Valhalla: the god Odin's hall, where slain warriors feasted after death

Valkyries: thirteen maidens who served Odin and took dead warriors from earth's battlefields to Valhalla

Vanir: deities of wealth, fertility, and pleasure

volva: a woman who was a prophet or seer

wattle and daub: branches interwoven within a framework and covered with mud or clay to make a wall

wergild: a fine paid to the victim of a crime or the victim's family by the person who committed the crime; the amount of the fine was set according to the victim's social rank.

Yggdrasil (IG-druh-sill)**:** the World Tree, whose branches and roots supported the nine worlds of Viking mythology

FOR FURTHER READING

Branston, Brian. *Gods and Heroes from Viking Mythology.* New York: Peter Bedrick, 1994.

Carter, Avis Murton. *One Day with the Vikings.* New York: Abelard-Schuman, 1974.

Charnan, Simon. *Leif Eriksson and the Vikings.* Chicago: Children's Press, 1991.

Civardi, Anne, and James Graham-Campbell. *The Time Traveller Book of Viking Raiders.* London: Usborne, and Tulsa: EDC, 1990.

Climo, Shirley. *Stolen Thunder: A Norse Myth.* New York: Clarion Books, 1994.

Cohat, Yves. *The Vikings, Lords of the Seas.* New York: Abrams, 1992.

Glubok, Shirley. *The Art of the Vikings.* New York: Macmillan, 1978.

Golding, Morton J. *The Mystery of the Vikings in America.* Philadelphia and New York: J. B. Lippincott, 1973.

Hook, Jason. *The Vikings.* New York: Thomson Learning, 1993.

Humble, Richard. *The Age of Leif Eriksson.* New York: Franklin Watts, 1989.

MacDonald, Fiona. *Vikings.* New York: Barrons, 1992.

MacDonald, Fiona. *A Viking Town.* New York: Peter Bedrick, 1995.

Martell, Hazel. *The Vikings and Jorvik.* New York: Dillon Press, 1993.

Martell, Hazel. *What Do We Know About the Vikings?* New York: Peter Bedrick, 1992.

Mayer, Marianna. *Iduna and the Magic Apples.* New York: Macmillan, 1988.

Morley, Jacqueline. *First Facts About the Vikings.* New York: Peter Bedrick, 1996.

Nicholson, Robert, and Claire Watts. *The Vikings: Facts, Stories, and Activities*. New York and Philadelphia: Chelsea Juniors, 1994.

Philip, Neil. *Odin's Family: Myths of the Vikings*. New York: Orchard Books, 1996.

Pruneti, Luigi. *Viking Explorers*. New York: Peter Bedrick, 1995.

Wingate, Philippa, and Dr. Anne Millard. *The Viking World*. London: Usborne, and Tulsa: EDC, 1993.

BIBLIOGRAPHY

Almgren, Bertil, et al. *The Viking*. New York: Crescent Books, 1972.

Aswynn, Freya. *Leaves of Yggdrasil*. St. Paul: Llewellyn, 1990.

Auden W. H., and Paul B. Taylor. *Norse Poems*. London: Athlone Press, 1981.

Bellows, Henry Adams, trans. *The Poetic Edda*. 1923. Reprint, New York: Biblo and Tannen, 1969.

Editors of Time-Life Books. *Vikings: Raiders from the North*. Alexandria, Virginia: Time-Life Books, 1993.

Graham-Campbell, James, ed. *Cultural Atlas of the Viking World*. New York: Facts on File, 1994.

James, Peter, and Nick Thorpe. *Ancient Inventions*. New York: Ballantine Books, 1994.

Jones, Gwyn. *A History of the Vikings.* rev. ed. Oxford and New York: Oxford University Press, 1984.

Jordan, Robert Paul. "Viking Trail East." *National Geographic,* 169, no. 3 (March 1985).

La Fay, Howard. *The Vikings.* Washington: National Geographic Society, 1972.

Levathes, Louise. "Iceland: Life under the Glaciers." *National Geographic,* 171, no. 2 (February 1987).

Lindow, John. "Riddles, Kennings, and the Complexity of Skaldic Poetry." *Scandinavian Studies,* 46, no. 3 (no date).

Magnusson, Magnus. *Vikings!* New York: Elsevier-Dutton, 1980.

Marsden, John. *The Fury of the Northmen.* New York: St. Martin's Press, 1993.

Roesdahl, Else. *The Vikings!* Translated by Susan M. Margeson and Kirsten Williams. London and New York: Penguin Books, 1991.

Sturluson, Snorri. *The Prose Edda: Tales from Norse Mythology.* Translated by Jean I. Young. Berkeley and Los Angeles: University of California Press, 1954.

Turville-Petre, G. "Scaldic Poetry: History and Literature." In *Bibliography of Old Norse-Icelandic Studies 1969,* edited by Hans Bekker-Nielsen. Copenhagen, 1970.

INDEX

Page numbers for illustrations are in boldface

ABOUT THE AUTHOR

When Kathryn Hinds was a child, her Swedish grandfather entertained her with stories of the Vikings and their daring voyages, and she has been interested in the Vikings ever since. Ms. Hinds grew up near Rochester, New York, then moved to New York City to study music and writing at Barnard College. She did graduate work in comparative literature at the City University of New York, where she enjoyed taking a course in Old Norse. For several years she has worked as a freelance editor of children's books. She also writes poetry, which has been published in a number of magazines. Ms. Hinds now lives in the north Georgia mountains with her husband, their son, a dog, and a varying number of cats. Her other books in this series are *The Incas, The Ancient Romans, The Celts of Northern Europe,* and *India's Gupta Dynasty.*